Praise for *Forever Unforgivable*

Brent MacDonald draws from the deep wells of servant-leader to the underserved, devoted Christ-follower, disciplined student of the Word, Director of a nationally recognized, pace-setting ministry, and devoted husband and father. He's the real deal. And then he writes this book... Forever Unforgivable is a gut check, a cliché killer. It will call you to reevaluate your practice of faith in the unlimited reach and power of Christ's forgiveness. The Church has needed this book for a long time. 'Seems the Lord had Brent MacDonald deliver it at just the right time.

Bob Landham

Missions Pastor, New Vision Baptist Church

Murfreesboro, Tennessee, USA

Brent's scholarly research infused with his historical and geographical expertise brings to life several extreme stories of seemingly unforgivable people whose lives were transformed by God's amazing grace! This informative, thought provoking book will be kept on my shelf as a reference for Bible study and illustrations.

Jackie Redmond

RESOUND NOW, Executive Director

Knoxville, TN, USA

Brent MacDonald has truly captured the essence of the marvelous grace and forgiveness of Almighty God. His forgiveness is nothing cheap or casual. It comes at the highest price possible—the sacrifice of His Son Jesus Christ. That perfect blood sacrifice can wash away sins, even the worst we could imagine along with those written for us by Brent, IF the sinner is willing to accept what Jesus did for him/her and enter into a relationship with Christ that is clearly life changing.

Brent certainly challenges all readers, believers and not-yet believers, to dig deep into one's soul to answer such provoking questions found throughout the book and particularly at the end. It all boils down to whether or not we believe God has the right to forgive even the worst of all sinners. Like Paul, some of us may find that we qualify/qualified to be chief among them.

Ron Chaffee

United Methodist Pastor, retired

Maine, USA

Creativity and historical research are two tools that Brent MacDonald has skillfully employed as he endeavors to bring life into the characters portrayed in his new book "Forever Unforgiveable." He has taken characters that many of us thought we knew, and some that we hope we never know, and put flesh back on their bones and made them people again. The result of his labor is easy to read and personally challenging at the same time.

It is hard to miss the theme of the book, as we think of the forgiveness of those "people we hope to never know." Brent continues to drive home the deeper question "Are we willing to forgive as we have been forgiven and to love the way God has called us to love?" And it is not a rhetorical question. It demands an answer from each one of us individually and as the body of Christ's Church here on earth. Brent challenges the reader to understand the truth that "If forgiveness is what we seek for ourselves, then it must be what we are willing to offer to others."

Dave McPherson

Pastor, New Canaan Baptist Church

New Brunswick, Canada


Forgiveness is a dominant theme throughout the Bible and does not always come easy for Christians to extend. Brent's writing provides an easy to read and practical resource for wrestling through the subject of forgiveness. 15 stories and at the end of each one I paused and asked myself what would I do? Each story will challenge you to consider your response.

Whether you are a new believer or a seasoned saint the question that arises is how far can/should/would I go in forgiving a vile sinner. The topic of forgiveness has always been a very relevant topic but especially today when our society seems to hold people hostage to their past.

Donald Calder

Lead Pastor, Temple Baptist Church

Sarnia, Ontario, Canada


*Forever Unforgiveable* is a work written in a unique way that presents the contents with freshness and clarity that captures the reader's attention from beginning to end. Brent MacDonald writes to communicate that no grievous sinner, whatever gross level the sinner might have reached, is beyond God's mercies and grace for redemption and transformation.

The stories of each grace recipient, whether biblical or non-biblical characters, are presented in a concise and non-complex manner that renders technical data easily comprehensible for the reader. This book is a must read especially in these times of profiling individuals based on race, origins, society class, and cultural orientation. It is a must read for the times.

Dr. Rodney Masona

Principal, Baptist Theological Seminary of Zambia

Lusaka, Zambia

Here is a book that brings us astonishing stories of the lives of individuals of varying backgrounds, spanning from the time Christ walked the earth to our present day. As each of the characters encountered Jesus Christ, their lives became profound demonstrations of the power and grace of God and they became powerful witnesses for His kingdom. One of the persons in this book (my first Bible teacher) had a profound effect on my life. What a delight to "meet" him again in the pages of this book and to learn of his encounter with Christ!

This powerful book, brilliantly written, with fascinating background and vivid testimonies showing the power of Almighty God who changes lives, will impact others for eternity. The author has given us hope during these despairing times. A must read for Christians and non-Christians alike.

Sudesh Gordhandass Valji

Pastor, Upper Kingsclear, New Brunswick

New Brunswick, Canada

# Forever Unforgivable

Learning to forgive the
inexcusable for Christ's sake

Brent J. MacDonald

Published by Kharis Publishing, imprint of Kharis Media LLC.

Copyright © 2019 by Brent MacDonald

ISBN-13: 978-1-946277-70-1
ISBN-10: 1-946277-70-3
Library of Congress Control Number: 2020943671

All enquiries or order requests, should be directed to:

Kharis Media LLC

Tel: 1-479-599-8657

support@kharispublishing.com

www.kharispublishing.com

# Acknowledgements

This book wouldn't be possible without the patient input of my wife, Angie. Her feedback on possible ideas and wording through every draft is an invaluable aid in crafting a finished work. My penchant for writing at odd hours frequently meant interruptions of her sleep.

Thanks to Debbie Fortune and Allen Barnes for their text proofing, helpful corrections, and suggestions for clarifying footnotes.

Thanks to my son, Scott, a missionary in Zambia, Africa, for suggesting the chapter on Byang Kato and sourcing the documents necessary for my research.

# Content

# Introduction

Imagine hearing breaking news that Hassan Nasrallah[1], the longtime head of the militant terrorist organization Hezbollah has dramatically become a Christian believer. And now, your government has granted him amnesty and asylum to keep his former compatriots from ending him. On Sunday morning, you find out that Hassan is attending your church and he's now living in your community. How will you react to this man, responsible for the deaths of so many, as he sits next to you in the Sunday morning service or comes to your small group fellowship? Would you be angry with the Christian brother or sister who invited him to come?

In the following weeks, what if he spots you while you're at a restaurant with coworkers? Would you try to look away or return his recognition? And what if he comes to your table to say hello? Would you introduce him as a friend? As a believer in Jesus Christ, how would you react? Would you want the world to see you with this man?

Our modern western world with its hashtag movements easily answers these questions.[2] We live in a time

---

[1] For my introduction's theoretical example, I selected a major terrorist figure that perhaps will be alive when you read this. The example works with any currently at-large living terrorist you can think of. Most end up dead or permanently imprisoned.

[2] #justice #racism #humanrights #women #activism #issues

when mere accusation of former wrongdoing leads to vilifying and ostracizing people. Finding out that someone did something twenty-five years ago, or merely suspect that someone did, and social media (if not the press) will have them condemned and denigrated publicly. The years since the proven or alleged misdeeds don't matter, nor does the individual's present behavior. Simply put, "once a bad person, always a bad person." These persistent public voices give no choice and we're told we must agree. Their constant and continuing message demands we endlessly condemn and shun all such evil people. In pursuit of social justice, we're told we must silence or avoid even people tainted by their association with these evildoers.

What about Christ's church? We're different from the world, aren't we? If we find no difference, more questions arise: Does the Bible speak to this subject? Should believers, the church,[3] be different in what we believe and how we act?

**Ephesians 4:31** Let all bitterness and wrath and anger and clamor and slander be put away from you, along with all malice. 32 Be kind to one another, tenderhearted, forgiving one another, as God in Christ forgave you. 5:1 Therefore be imitators of God, as beloved children.

---

#socialjustice #issues #care

[3] The Greek word for church, ecclesia, has nothing to do with a building or meeting place. It's "the called-out ones," meaning all believers in Jesus Christ, the congregation.

# Chapter One

## How Bad is Bad?

When considering evil people, it's easy to start mentally listing what we feel to be seriously bad. Racists, murderers, human traffickers, terrorists, rapists, jihadis, the list is long. These days society considers bad far more than convicted criminals, it's anyone whose behavior or beliefs we feel are "criminal" that makes a person bad.[4] Others redefine and expand the word's definition to include any person on the wrong side of politics, or questioning "settled" science, or opposing popular public opinion (...whatever that is today).[5]

God wants His church to have a better and unchanging definition of bad. Unlike the world, which mostly believes ideas of good and bad evolved, we have a fixed standard. Our perfect and good God defined sin for us.[6] The

---

[4] At the same time modern society had redefined good and bad, but this is another issue. Consider Isaiah 5:20-21.

[5] Disagreeing with popular science may not have you physically put to death, but non-belief in its doctrines can certainly lead to your academic death and termination of any public career.

[6] Luke 18:19b No one is good except God alone. (Also see Matthew 5:48 and Psalms 18:30).

Bible clearly states or defines certain behaviors and thoughts as wickedness. While some sins are plainly more severe, such as murder and sexual sins (because they affect multiple lives), the Bible makes clear that even so-called "little" sins deserve Divine capital punishment.

**Romans 6:23a** For the wages of sin is death…

Most breathe a sigh of relief that they've hidden their wrongdoings more successfully than those newsworthy evildoers or people formally convicted of a crime. Others find comfort in their belief that their sins "aren't that bad." It's easy to condemn or look down on people seemingly worse, or perhaps stupid enough to get caught.

Proper perspective comes from God's word which reminds us that He knows everything about all of us:

**Hebrews 4:13** Nothing in all creation is hidden from God's sight. Everything is uncovered and laid bare before the eyes of him to whom we must give account. (NIV)

Great or small, each of us has thoughts and deeds that we hope will never see the light of day. Imagine if someone suddenly exposed your worst, even if it was from decades ago. How might your family or the world react to the unquestionable video of those long-ago actions? How would other believers in your church respond? While it offers no excuse, the longer each of us was an unbeliever, the longer we had to live driven by selfish desires. Before coming to faith in Jesus Christ, we also lived in the thoughts and actions of our sinful nature.

**Ephesians 2:1** As for you, you were dead in your transgressions and sins, 2 in which you used to live when you followed the ways of this world and of the ruler of the kingdom of the air, the spirit who is now at work in those who are disobedient. 3 All of us also lived among them at one time, gratifying the cravings of our sinful nature and following its desires and thoughts. Like the rest, we were by nature objects of wrath. 4 But because of his great love for us, God, who is rich in mercy, **5** made us alive with Christ even when we were dead in transgressions—it is by grace you have been saved. **6** And God raised us up with Christ and seated us with him in the heavenly realms in Christ Jesus, **7** in order that in the coming ages he might show the incomparable riches of his grace, expressed in his kindness to us in Christ Jesus. **8** For it is by grace you have been saved, through faith—and this not from yourselves, it is the gift of God— **9** not by works, so that no one can boast. **10** For we are God's workmanship, created in Christ Jesus to do good works, which God prepared in advance for us to do. (NIV)

Paul's Ephesian letter reminds us that even a person once consumed by wickedness can find transformation in Jesus Christ. Their new life is far different from their former life, with God-enabled good works now central. We Christians claim to recognize this truth, but do we live it? More than mentally consenting to the truth that God redeems wicked people, our words and actions display whether we truly believe this. Do we accept them? Do we socialize with them? Do we encourage them? Are we willing to appear publicly with these men and women?

Are you willing to appear with a former murderer, a prior human trafficker, or a past racist? If you're not, heaven will surely disappoint because the crowd around God's throne will include these people and worse.

I've selected fifteen examples of historically vile men and women. I expect revulsion will be your reaction to reading some of their early deeds. You may have trouble considering the enormity of their crimes. Their early actions are unquestionably disgusting and despicable. Though many more cases exist, consider these six individuals chosen from regular historical records and seven from the Bible's inspired ancient accounts.[7] Each chosen person later became a believer, a

---

[7] In all my chosen examples I've attempted to remain faithful to known historical details, sometimes supplementing biblical examples with extra-biblical historical information. As necessary, some

10

Christian, by the grace of God. From that moment onward every believer they met had a choice. Whether personally or corporately: Do you reject or accept this man or woman? It's not enough to *say*, "God forgives and accepts." The Bible gives no halfway position; we must forgive and accept too.

**Matthew 6:14** For if you forgive others their trespasses, your heavenly Father will also forgive you, **15** but if you do not forgive others their trespasses, neither will your Father forgive your trespasses.

Some will ask another question as they read these accounts: "Can you guarantee these people became believers?" In asking this question some seek a way out, another way to slyly reject these individuals. In return, another question must be asked. Can you guarantee your spouse is a believer, your friend from church, or even your pastor? Why do you accept them but are willing to reject another repentant sinner and now saved believer? God alone can guarantee someone is a believer:

**2 Timothy 2:19** But God's firm foundation stands, bearing this seal: "The Lord knows those who are his," and, "Let everyone who names the name of the Lord depart from iniquity."

In some of our selected examples God openly guarantees this individual became a believer. Yet, God rarely reveals other's faith with certainty to other people. God didn't provide this assurance to most people that knew those scriptural individuals in their time. As 2 Timothy 2:19 implies, we see an individual's rejection of wickedness as evidence of conversion, a result of God's salvation. The longer we know someone, the greater we should see the fruit of God's Holy Spirit at work in their lives. It's natural for us to question whether someone's salvation is real and perhaps to fear them

---

reasonable inferences are employed. While Old Testament examples abound, I've limited my biblical examples to the New Testament, each clearly showing the selected individual coming to faith in the incarnate or resurrected Messiah.

for what they once were.[8] We want to hold off on any acceptance until we can examine *enough* fruit. While it is God that gives fruit to His people, He also created the church to nurture those people so they can grow more fruit. This means there is much watering and pruning needed before there are even buds and blossoms, let alone fruit. God commands us to get in there and work with a new believer long before a harvest of righteousness is fully visible. We can only hope God grants us time to witness their fruit:

**Galatians 5:22** But the fruit of the Spirit is love, joy, peace, patience, kindness, goodness, faithfulness, [23] gentleness and self-control. Against such things there is no law. [24] Those who belong to Christ Jesus have crucified the sinful nature with its passions and desires.

The fruit of a changed life is readily visible for some people we examine but limited for those whose lives God cut short. Either way, we accept their declaration of belief and find assurance of their conversion in their briefly seen fruit.[9]

---

[8] Ananias questioned God over the safety of accepting Saul as a new believer, only going because God again commanded him to do so. See Acts 9:10-17. We consider Saul's life late in this book.

[9] The repentant thief crucified alongside Jesus had limited time to exhibit spiritual fruit, but there was some. See Luke 23:32-43

# Chapter Two

## Officers in an Occupying Army

Rape, murder, human trafficking, involuntary servitude, unjust taxes, corruption: This is a fitting list of crimes attributable tall Roman army participants. [10] If a soldier didn't

---

[10] Under Caesar, officer ranks from highest to lowest:

- Legatus Augusti proparetore (highest rank senior officers and regional military governors, from Rome's senatorial class).
- Tribunus laticlavius (senatorial class second level senior officers).
- Legatus legionis (senatorial class commander of a legion, or ten cohorts).
- Praefecti (equestrian rank officers over a cavalry unit).
- Tribunus Anticlavius or Tribunus Augusticlavii (equestrian rank officers, one of five in each legion).
- Praefectus castrorum (equestrian rank officers, the camp prefect or administrator).
- Centurion (lowest rank equestrian officer or highest rank ordinary soldier, commander of 80 - 100 men).
- Principales – Optio (centurion's second in command).
- Principales – Signifer (the unit's standard bearer).

personally commit each themselves, they unquestionably had

knowledge of compatriots who did, or they directly aided and encouraged others in commission of these crimes. Commanding officers were equally culpable for their own actions and their subordinates.

I've selected two examples, one from scripture and another from the many volumes of Roman history passed down to us. Both men called Caesarea by the Sea[11] home, at least for a time. This coastal city was a monument to the building genius of the despotic Roman collaborator King Herod. The first officer we'll consider is Cornelius. By his time, around 40 AD, Rome had direct control over Judea with Caesarea as the provincial capital. This city included Jews and Gentiles – indeed, everyone wanting to be close to the highest political powers called this city home.

The Roman army was the muscle behind this foreign occupying government. Rome's *procurator*, or governor, had the final say on all life and death matters under Caesar himself. Only Roman citizens could choose to appeal his judgment to Caesar.

## Cornelius

Cornelius was a centurion, one of six in his cohort,

---

- Principales – Tesserarius (guard commander).

[11] Also known as Caesarea Maritima. The "Maritima" or "By the Sea" designation was necessary to distinguish this coastal city from another called Caesarea in northern Israel near Mount Hermon, specifically Caesarea Philippi, also named in honor of Caesar by Herod Philip II.

personally in charge of about 100 men. His regiment was the Cohors II Miliaria Italica Civium Romanorum Voluntariorum, more succinctly called the Italian Cohort by Luke in the book of Acts.[12] Unlike the multitude of infantry cohorts, everyone in this specialized unit was an archer. Caesar originally formed the Italian Cohort in Rome from freed slaves who had received their citizenship. It wasn't a regular Legionary unit, but rather an Auxiliary one. Officials normally recruited Auxiliaries from noncitizens and they especially used provincial volunteers. Cornelius was a foreign *voluntarii* who had done well rising through the ranks of this specialist cohort.

Jews never feared conscription or enticement into Rome's army as the Emperor exempted such service from the time of Augustus onward. This exemption was a reasonable concession by Roman authorities. Jews, with their strict belief in one Creator and invisible God, would never fit in with polytheistic Roman units. These soldiers worshiped many Roman gods and idols, plus there was regular observance of the cult of Deified Caesar. All cohorts repeatedly paraded images and symbols of these gods, including the current Emperor.

Rising to the rank of centurion guaranteed Cornelius was a polytheist publicly making offerings to Caesar. No one doubted his bravery and skill as his years of success in battles and skirmishes had singled him out for promotion. The 3-foot-long wooden vine-branch cudgel Cornelius carried wasn't merely a measure of his rank. His men feared his discipline. The army tasked him with keeping order among the unruly rabble that commonly volunteered for these regiments. Aside from joining with the hope of gaining Roman citizenship and land (at retirement), these individuals enlisted to seek plunder and gratify their baser instincts in their brutal conquests of Caesar's enemies.

While we don't know how long Rome had kept

---

[12] Acts 10:1  At Caesarea there was a man named Cornelius, a centurion of what was known as the Italian Cohort.

Cornelius stationed at Caesarea, something had happened to him during his time there. This brutal polytheistic occupier became sympathetic to the people whom he had been tasked with controlling. The last few years of his service were under the Emperor Gaius Julius Caesar Germanicus, better known by his longtime nickname Caligula, meaning "little boot." Cornelius had witnessed his supreme commander's increasing hostility toward these monotheistic Jews. In fact, Caligula became the first emperor who intended for the Jews to add his image to their Jerusalem temple. Cornelius witnessed the bravery of the Jews and their willingness to sacrifice themselves in order to protect their faith and holy sites. He was henceforth persuaded that the Jewish creator God was the only true God and that all the gods of Rome were false ones.[13] His new understanding of false gods included Caesar Caligula – the volatile self-professed god who delighted in watching torture and executions, often spending his nights in orgies of gluttony and unbridled sexual passions. Rumors abounded that this Roman god was merely an insane man.

While most Jews would never accept him as anything more than a sympathetic God-fearer, Cornelius resolved to help these people through his gifts to their ever-present poor and needy. Most of all, Cornelius sought to know God and committed himself to continually pray to Him.

God answered Cornelius' prayers, sending the Apostle Peter to him to fully reveal this triune God he was seeking to know.[14] Not only was Peter a Jew who should never have been socializing with an unclean Gentile, Peter was aware Cornelius' job included oppressing the Jewish people. Cornelius represented this madman Emperor who planned to defile the temple and city of Jerusalem by forcing the people to worship him as god. And yet, God showed Peter it didn't matter that

---

[13] Acts 10:2 a devout man who feared God with all his household, gave alms generously to the people, and prayed continually to God.

[14] The entire account of God sending Peter and his subsequent interaction with Cornelius appears in Acts 10:1 – 11:18.

Cornelius was a Gentile. It didn't matter that he represented the occupying state. It didn't matter that this man was formerly responsible for atrocities and murders. Peter was to accept Cornelius because God now accepted him.

It was equally irrelevant what Jews in Caesarea thought or how those in the early Jewish faith viewed this man; Peter was obedient to God and entered this man's house. And through his obedience he saw many of Cornelius' household also come to faith in Jesus Christ. Yes, this once vile murdering oppressor was now publicly a brother in Christ – the first Gentile convert – and a welcoming home for believers whether Jew or Gentile.

We don't know the end of Cornelius' military career. While he had already served for many years, his commitment was for a twenty-five-year term. This was his sworn and unbreakable contract. In the following years, apostles and other visiting Christian brothers and sisters came to visit with Cornelius. Yes, they were visiting and socializing with someone who remained a soldier in the Roman army. In order for Cornelius to manage his duties in clear conscience before God, he would have strived to be the best soldier he could be – as someone who kept his lawful oaths. But this was likely done at personal detriment as he could no longer offer sacrifices to Caesar or honor the Roman legionary gods. Unquestionably, a hostile opponent would use this open knowledge to their personal advantage.

## Marinus

Two centuries later,[15] God was still calling and saving Roman soldiers at Caesarea. This growth came through the efforts of Christians willing to visit with and share God's good news with these Roman occupiers. In the ranks of Caesarea's Roman cohort, Marinus became a believer in Jesus Christ.[16]

---

[15] Around 262 AD.

[16] The historical accuracy of this account rests with its

Though the Emperor Gallienus ruled in Rome a usurper named Macrianus Major recently declared himself ruler in the east empire. [17]

Marinus' fellow soldiers knew he was a Christian believer. His sharing this was perhaps made easier by the Emperor Gallienus' formal declaration of tolerance of Christians.[18] But, only a short time later, Marinus' emperor and supreme commander was now the intolerant Macrianus. The *legatus legionis* sided with Macrianus, so all lesser soldiers had no choice but to also follow his lead. Yet, Macrianus was openly hostile to Christians and now the Palestinian tribunals answered to him.

As a Christian, Marinus wasn't an oath breaker and he continued to honor his military commitment, even though the present ruler was a wicked oppressor of Christians.[19] Everyone

---

contemporaneous source: the history of Eusebius of Caesarea, also known as Eusebius Pamphili. Eusebius was an early church historian and bishop of Caesarea Maritima, around 314 AD, about 50 years after the event described. This esteemed Caesarean resident published his account while eyewitnesses to the described events were still alive.

[17] Around 260 AD.

[18] In 259 AD.

[19] 1 Corinthians 7:20 Each one should remain in the condition in which he was called. [21] Were you a bondservant when called? Do not

knew Marinus to be a brave, honorable, and capable man, one who served well. By order of succession, he was next in line to wield the vine-branch as the previous centurion completed his service. Immediately, another veteran soldier in Marinus' *centuria*, who resented this Christian soldier, petitioned the military tribunal. He appeared before the tribunal claiming it wasn't legal for Marinus to receive such a dignity and his belief the centurion's office should belong to him. His sole charge against Marinus was that as a Christian he wouldn't make a sacrifice to their new emperor as god. The tribunal judge called Marinus before him to answer for himself. When asked, Marinus quickly and publicly confirmed himself a Christian.[20]

The Roman judge, Achaeus, not wanting to disqualify this honorable and capable soldier, gave him three hours for reflection and an opportunity to recant. The local pastor, Theotecnus, spent this time with him – willing to publicly identify with his brother in Christ. Setting a copy of the gospels before him, the pastor pointed to the soldier's sword and the Scriptures before him, telling Marinus to choose between the two. Marinus, without hesitation, reached out his right hand and clasped the divine. Theotecnus then reminded him "Hold fast, then, hold fast to God and strengthened by Him may you obtain what you have chosen..." With three hours now passed, a herald summoned Marinus to again appear before the tribunal. Here he confirmed himself a follower of Jesus Christ. The official judgment was swift. Rather than a temporary elevation to the office of centurion and its accompanying

---

be concerned about it. (But if you can gain your freedom, avail yourself of the opportunity.) [22] For he who was called in the Lord as a bondservant is a freedman of the Lord. Likewise he who was free when called is a bondservant of Christ. [23] You were bought with a price; do not become bondservants of men. [24] So, brothers, in whatever condition each was called, there let him remain with God.

[20] Marinus lived out Matthew 10:32 So everyone who acknowledges me before men, I also will acknowledge before my Father who is in heaven, [33] but whoever denies me before men, I also will deny before my Father who is in heaven.

honor, soldiers led Marinus away to honor his Lord by his death.

The church of Marinus' day was willing to associate with this now godly man. Regardless of his earlier deeds, he was now a believer in Jesus Christ and a willing and unwavering martyr for his faith.

# Chapter Three

## Racists – Murderers and Human Traffickers

### John Newton

John Newton's childhood was rough. Born in 1725 London to a godly Christian mother, she died two weeks before his seventh birthday from tuberculosis. John's father quickly remarried, and life grew worse for John because of his poor connection with his new stepmother. In response, at age 8, John's father sent him to boarding school, his first experience with formal schooling. This lasted for two years, when his father, a stern no-nonsense merchant sea captain, took him to sea at age eleven. He quickly succumbed to negative influences common to rabble seafarers and descended into a reckless life of drinking and carousing.

Everyone knew John for his vulgar and blasphemous speech, profanity, and "unsettled behavior and impatience of restraint." As was common in eighteenth century England, the British Navy forcibly recruited him[21] to serve on a Navy vessel

---

[21] Forcible recruitment of seamen into the British Navy is officially known as "press gang." Those press-ganged into the Navy were often given no notice and were mostly merchant seamen rounded up on the docks of England. The British Navy justified this conscription practice to keep their Navy, the backbone of the British Empire, at peak strength. These hastily drafted recruits had no choice and no recourse and could be charged with desertion for abandoning their

(in 1744). He predictably rebelled against military discipline and deserted. When caught, the captain had him flogged, with John receiving eight dozen lashes and was confined in irons. Somehow, he convinced his superiors to rid themselves of him through a transfer to a slaver ship. Life on a slaver ship wasn't much better and his new masters treated him cruelly.

Amid all the surrounding depravity, Newton arrogantly remained insubordinate and embraced moral abandon. He later wrote of this period, "I sinned with a high hand and I made it my study to tempt and seduce others." Again, the ship's captain transferred this almost useless sailor to another ship. During this ship's return voyage to England a fierce storm overtook the vessel off the coast of Ireland.

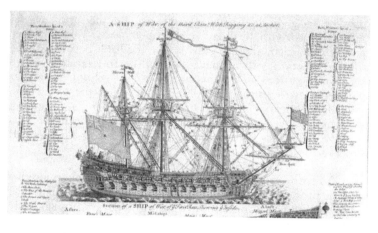

The disabled ship, Greyhound, nearly sank. With torn sails and one side of the ship splintered, all the sailors worked the pumps trying to keep the vessel afloat. By the eleventh day, Newton was so exhausted he could no longer man a pump, so the crew lashed him against the helm and tasked him with trying to hold the ship on course. It was during these eleven harrowing hours that Newton remembered Proverbs 1:24-30...

ship.

**Proverbs 1:24** Because I have called and you refused to listen, have stretched out my hand and no one has heeded, ²⁵ because you have ignored all my counsel and would have none of my reproof, ²⁶ I also will laugh at your calamity; I will mock when terror strikes you, ²⁷ when terror strikes you like a storm and your calamity comes like a whirlwind, when distress and anguish come upon you. ²⁸ Then they will call upon me, but I will not answer; they will seek me diligently but will not find me. ²⁹ Because they hated knowledge and did not choose the fear of the LORD, ³⁰ would have none of my counsel and despised all my reproof...

Newton, in fear of his life and soul, called on God to save him. He saw God's mercy and miraculous hand in how the cargo miraculously shifted to seal the hole in the ship's hull allowing the vessel finally to drift to safety. John marked this day in March of 1748 as his conversion to Christianity.

Many allege a radical and immediate transformation in Newton's behavior as they tell Newton's story. Yet, this now professing Christian didn't radically change his ways overnight. He afterwards became a ship's mate and later captain himself, yet still serving the slave trade. Indeed, this declared Christian continued as a racist human trafficker. He admitted conditions onboard the slaver ship were atrocious often leading to slave deaths:

"[The slaves] are kept down, by the weather, to breathe a hot and corrupted air, sometimes for a week: this, added to the galling of their irons, and the despondency which seizes their spirits, when thus confined, soon becomes fatal."[22]

As the shipmate, he recorded how many died on one journey from Africa to South Carolina and what the loss meant for the slave trade as a whole:

"The ship, in which I was mate, left the coast with two hundred and eighteen slaves on board; and though we were not much affected by epidemical disorders, I find, by my journal of that voyage (now before me) that we buried sixty-two on our passage to South Carolina, exclusive of those which died before we left the coast, of which I have no account. I believe, upon an average between the more healthy, and the more sickly voyages, and including all contingencies, One fourth of the whole purchase may be allotted to the article of mortality. That is, if the English ships purchase sixty thousand slaves annually, upon the whole extent of the coast, the annual loss of lives cannot be much less than fifteen thousand."[23]

John was an admitted accomplice in the death of multitudes. But he was now a slave trader reading and learning from God's word. He first justified his continued actions and career believing he could be a better slave trader by restraining slave trade "excesses." He also believed he could "promote the life of God in the soul" to his crew and African cargo. John would later recognize how misguided he was during that period: "I cannot consider myself to have been a believer, in the full sense of the word, until a considerable time afterwards." And yet, despite his continued sin, God was at work in his life.

This Christian captain continued to sell his fellow human beings for three voyages, the last taking him to the Caribbean island of St. Kitts. It was in St. Kitts John met someone different...

-----

[22] Published in The Scots Magazine, Volume 50, 1788.

[23] Published in The Scots Magazine, Volume 50, 1788.

"a brother shipper, his name is Alexander Clunie, he is a tall Christian."

This was Newton's way of saying that this colleague and captain (who traded in gunpowder, not humankind) was a strong believer. Remember, John Newton wasn't eloquent and had a limited vocabulary from his two years of formal schooling. There in St. Kitts, he then regularly attended St. Anne's Church. He grew so much in his faith that this church wanted to hire him as their pastor.

It was at St. Kitts where John suffered a stroke, which occurred in 1754. He credited God with saving him from death during this serious health scare. His friend, Alexander Clunie, counseled John to not accept the pastorate here, but rather to return to England and grow further in his faith. John took Clunie's advice, returning to England, and retired from the sea for a career as a customs officer in 1755. While no longer personally a slave trader, Newton still invested in the slave trade during this time.

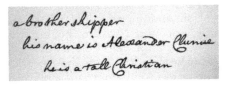

No longer at sea, John began to host Bible studies in his Liverpool home. Having now already learned Latin[24], Newton now taught himself Greek, Syriac[25], and Hebrew to aid in his biblical studies. As his Bible knowledge grew

---

[24] Latin was commonly used by scholars in his day.

[25] Biblical Aramaic

exponentially, so too did his disgust for the slave trade and his former and present role in it.

Quitting his office job, Newton sought ordination in the Anglican church resulting in officials summarily rejecting his petition. Through his persistence, the church finally granted ordination and assigned him a rural parish in 1764. Newton was unlike most 18th century English preachers, who were typically distant from their parishioners and seemingly aloof from sin and temptation. Instead, everyone knew John for his personal involvement in his congregation's lives and openly shared his own struggles and previous temptations and sins. In 1779, he moved to a new parish in London. Eight years later, Newton aided William Wilberforce's campaign to end slavery. His main contribution was writing "Thoughts Upon the African Slave Trade," for the first time openly condemning and expressing his revulsion over the former business he had once embraced.[26] A little over two years before his death in 1807, Newton declared[27]...

I am not what I ought to be! Ah! how imperfect and deficient! — I am not what I wish to be! I 'abhor what is evil,' and I would 'cleave to what is good!' — I am not what I hope to be! Soon, soon I shall put off mortality: and with mortality all sin and imperfection! Yet, though I am not what I ought to be, nor what I wish to be, nor what I hope to be, I can truly say, I am not what I once was — a slave to sin and Satan; and I can heartily join with the Apostle, and acknowledge, "By the grace of God I am what I am!"

---

[26] Written in 1787, *ThoughtUpon the African Slave Trade* was first published in 1788.

[27] As published in *The Christian Spectator*, Volume 3, 1821.

The public now best knows Newton, of course, as the writer of *Amazing Grace*, which he composed in 1772.[28] Christians worldwide sing this song, including former slaves and descendants of those former slaves. Members of his congregation were willing to identify with this repentant and transformed human trafficker, once steeped in sexual debauchery, drunkenness, and complicity in murder. Now that you know his story, are you willing to associate with this man and sing his song?[29]

Amazing grace! (How sweet the sound)
That saved a wretch like me!
I once was lost, but now am found;
Was blind, but now I see.

---

[28] *Amazing Grace* was written in 1772 and first published in 1779.

[29] Or any of the hundreds of other songs Newton wrote including *Glorious Things of Thee are Spoken.*

'Twas grace that taught my heart to fear,
And grace my fears relieved;
How precious did that grace appear
The hour I first believed!

Through many dangers, toils, and snares,
I have already come;
'Tis grace hath brought me safe thus far,
And grace will lead me home.

The LORD has promised good to me,
His word my hope secures;
He will my shield and portion be,
As long as life endures.

Yea, when this flesh and heart shall fail,
And mortal life shall cease,
I shall possess, within the veil,
A life of joy and peace.

The earth shall soon dissolve like snow,
The sun forbear to shine;
But GOD, who called me here below,
Will be forever mine.[30]

It's fitting that most singers commonly add a traditional African American stanza as a closing verse to Newton's original lyrics:

---

[30] Though later well-educated, Newton kept this song simple. Perhaps recalling his earlier life and formerly limited vocabulary, only twenty-one of the approximately 150 unique words used in this song have more than one syllable.

When we've been there ten thousand years,
Bright shining as the sun,
We've no less days to sing God's praise
Than when we'd first begun.[31]


## Nathan Bedford Forrest

Born in the United States almost 100 years after John Newton, Nathan Bedford Forrest also began life with a godly mother.[32] In this particular case, Nathan's mother lived, but his father died when he was only sixteen. Now as the "man of the house," he had ten younger siblings to care for. Life on the Tennessee frontier was rough and dangerous. Nathan didn't follow his mother's example. Though he rejected Christianity and neighbors knew him for cursing and gambling, he had integrity and honorably ran the family farm. Then, at age twenty-four, he shot and killed two Matlock brothers coming to collect a family debt. He stabbed the remaining two Matlock brothers, with only one surviving to tell the tale.

Though considered "backwoods" in nature, and uneducated, Nathan became a successful and well-off businessman. Fitting with his godless nature, he made his fortune as a racist slave trader, plus a cotton plantation owner.

---

[31] The original tune of Amazing Grace was never published and is long forgotten. In fact, the song was mostly forgotten for three or four decades. The American Second Great Awakening, especially in the revivals of the southern states of Kentucky and Tennessee in the early 19th century reintroduced the song's lyrics with at least twenty different tunes in use. In 1835, William Walker joined Newton's lyrics with the tune "New Britain," itself an amalgamation of two melodies earlier published by a pair of Kentucky college students.

[32] Nathan Bedford Forrest lived July 13, 1821 – October 29, 1877.

At the Civil War's onset, he was worth about 45 million dollars in present day equivalency.[33]

As the Civil War began in 1861, Nathan's home state of Tennessee and his current state of Mississippi both withdrew from the Union. With Nathan's passions and fortune tied to slavery, it was an easy choice for him to side with the Confederate States of America. He enlisted as a private in the cavalry and was so successful  that they promoted him to Lieutenant Colonel in his first year. His ambition and success saw him become the only man to rise from private to general during the Civil War. To the Union ``that devil Forrest" was a top public enemy, and reputedly the most skilled cavalryman the Civil War produced. It's reported that Ulysses S. Grant claimed to fear no earthly man except Nathan. Vicious in battle, Forrest killed thirty-one men in hand-to-hand combat, once taking on four Union soldiers simultaneously. He had thirty horses shot out from under him before the war ended. Though having no formal military training, generals considered him a genius military strategist.

---

[33] $1,500,000 in 1861 is equivalent in purchasing power to about $43,660,738.64 in 2019, a difference of $42,160,738.64 over 158 years. The buying power of $1,500,000 in 1861 is considered equivalent to $44,970,560.80 in 2020.

Though Forrest hadn't adopted his mother's Christian faith, he was respectful of Christianity and encouraged his troops to attend services. General Forrest often attended these services, as well. At home, Forrest remained faithfully devoted to his wife, a declared Christian he had married years earlier. He otherwise was visibly reputable, never disrespecting white women and often suppressing vulgar talk in his presence. He also didn't smoke or drink. Perhaps showing his true view of Christianity, he once referred to Christianity as a "women's religion." The fullness of Forrest's nature showed itself when he was mad. Some claimed his face would glow bright red and he became another person – and this person was famous for tirades laced with profanity.

Troops under Forrest's command were responsible for what became known as the Fort Pillow Massacre in April of 1864. While authorities would never personally hold Nathan responsible, his temper and hatred unquestionably played a great role in the operation. His personal orders started the charge on this Tennessee fort, with him commanding about 2000 soldiers against the fort's 600. One reason likely fueled his resolve to take this fort at all costs; the fort's final Union

Commander was Major William Bradford, a man that hailed from the same county of Tennessee as Forrest. Forrest, therefore, viewed Bradford as a traitor. His regiment now took the fort, even as its commander fled, with many soldiers now surrendering. Rules of war obliged Forrest's troops to treat surrendering soldiers as prisoners of war. Rather, Nathan's troops began shooting the surrendering soldiers on sight, the majority being black men, many former slaves. Forrest claimed it happened without his approval, as he only arrived on site twenty minutes after the fort had fallen. Because of his reputation over this incident northern citizens increasingly hated and feared Forrest.

LIEUTENANT GENERAL
NATHAN BEDFORD FORREST
1821 ••• 1877
CONFEDERATE STATES ARMY

Late in the war, in a rare moment when Nathan thought he might lose his life, he wrote a letter to his only son, Willie. In it, he asked his son to take care of his mother and to take care to not copy his sinful and wicked ways.

About a year later, after many Confederate generals had surrendered in 1865, Forrest too yielded. Merciful authorities allowed him to return home to his wife in Tennessee. Backing the wrong side reduced this formerly wealthy man to the $10 his wife Mary Ann had managed to save. Against his wife's wishes (who thought gambling a sin against God), Nathan quickly took all her money to a poker game and returned to his still unimpressed wife with $1,500.

Shortly after the war, a group of white men in Pulaski, Tennessee, founded the Ku Klux Klan; Forrest joined in 1867. This group was ostensibly a "protective" group for Southerners who feared the Northerners flooding the south for Reconstruction. Almost immediately upon joining the Klan, they elected Forrest as their first "Grand Wizard," forever tying him to Southern racism. He successfully worked to defeat Tennessee's pro-Union Governor in the polls of 1868, mostly through violence and intimidation and suppressing black and Republican voting rights. Forrest resigned from the Klan a year later (1869), claiming it was no longer necessary. At his departure, he ordered its dissolution and destruction of its costumes. Later, in Stone Mountain,

Georgia, the Klan of his day merely restructured and became the infamous violent organization that has terrorized blacks for decades to come.

In the early 1870's, now living in Memphis, Forrest began to attend a Presbyterian church with his wife, even as his health was now suffering from his lifetime of hard living and battles. Pastor George Stainback faithfully preached the gospel each Sunday and Nathan began to feel conviction for his life of sin. During this time, on the streets of Memphis, Nathan ran into a former army buddy, who had formerly been under his command. This man, Raleigh White, had already become a believer shortly after the war and was now a Southern Baptist pastor in Texas. After hearing Raleigh's testimony, Nathan asked if he would pray for him, which Raleigh immediately and publicly did in a bank lobby.

With Nathan and his wife present, a sermon by Pastor

Stainback, in the fall of 1875, focused on Jesus' words in Matthew 7:

**Matthew 7:24** "Everyone then who hears these words of mine and does them will be like a wise man who built his house on the rock. 25 And the rain fell, and the floods came, and the winds blew and beat on that house, but it did not fall, because it had been founded on the rock. 26 And everyone who hears these words of mine and does not do them will be like a foolish man who built his house on the sand. 27 And the rain fell, and the floods came, and the winds blew

REV. G. T. STAINBACK, D.D.

and beat against that house, and it fell, and great was the fall of it."

Following the service, Nathan spoke privately with the pastor, and with eyes filled with tears he confessed, "I am the fool that built on the sand; I am a poor miserable sinner." Pastor Stainback told him to go home and meditate on Psalms 51:

**Psalms 51:1** Have mercy on me, O God, according to your steadfast love; according to your abundant mercy blot out my transgressions. 2 Wash me thoroughly from my iniquity, and cleanse me from my sin! 3 For I know my transgressions, and my sin is ever before me.

The next evening the pastor visited Nathan and they prayed together. He had become a believer in Jesus Christ.[34]

That same year, an African American civil rights

---

[34] For a detailed account of Nathan's conversion, read *Nathan Bedford Forrest's Redemption* by Shane Kastler, 2010.

group[35] invited Forrest to speak. Though mocked by some white people for going, he went with the purpose of showing his changed heart. Forrest's address that evening was directly to his black listeners, most of those attending:

"I came here with the jeers of some white people, who think that I am doing wrong. I believe I can exert some influence and do much to assist the people in strengthening fraternal relations and shall do all in my power... to elevate every man, to depress none. I want to elevate you to take positions in law offices, in stores, on farms, and wherever you are capable of going. ... I came to meet you as friends and welcome you to the white people. I want you to come nearer to us. When I can serve you I will do so. We have but one flag, one country; let us stand together. We may differ in color, but not in sentiment. ... Go to work, be industrious, live honestly and act truly. And when you are oppressed, I'll come to your relief. I thank you, ladies and gentlemen, for this opportunity you have afforded me to be with you, and to assure you that I am with you in heart and in hand." [36]

Following Forrest's speech, a young black girl named Lou Lewis presented him with a bouquet of flowers as a visual symbol of their racial reconciliation. He not only accepted the flowers, but publicly and respectfully leaned down and kissed the black girl on the cheek – something unthinkable by a white man in that day.

Are you willing to identify with this brother in Christ, that came late to the Lord, this former murderer, slave trader and owner, and violent racist? Or are you like the world today that remembers Nathan Bedford Forrest only for his sins?

---

[35] The group was the *Independent Order of Pole-Bearers Association*, similar to today's NAACP.

[36] Excerpt from the *Memphis Daily Appeal*, July 6, 1875.

# Chapter Four

## Religiously Indifferent Pleasure Seekers

### Rachel of Sychar

Home, for Rachel,[37] was the village of Sychar.[38] Most outside the area hardly knew this place existed. The ruins of once great Shechem stood nearby. The Jewish Hasmonean ruler John Hyrcanus[39] destroyed that ancient great city, known to the patriarchs, Abraham, Isaac and Jacob.[40] Yes, the *Jews* had destroyed it! The name evoked only contempt. At least their new foreign oppressors, the Romans, protected Samaria's right to worship here on nearby Mount Gerizim.[41] For countless

---

[37] Scripture doesn't record this woman's name, so I chose for her a common regional name. Samaritans highly identified with the patriarch Jacob, who formerly lived in this area, so I picked "Rachel," the name of Jacob's beloved wife.

[38] See John 4:5.

[39] John Hyrcanus ruled from 134-104 BC. Shechem was destroyed in 107 BC.

[40] See Genesis 12:6, 33:18, 35:4, even 37:12-14.

[41] Mount Gerizim is one of the two mountains bordering biblical

generations the Jews had tried to force the Samaritans to abandon this "true" place of worship for that "false" Jewish temple in Jerusalem.[42] All Samaritans knew that God had decreed Mount Gerizim sacred when Israel entered the Promised Land – the place where God blessed His people.[43] Sadly, fifteen decades of hostile rulers prevented the Samaritans from rebuilding their former temple that once stood for hundreds of years on Mt. Gerizim. Hyrcanus was also responsible for the temple's destruction.[44] Even the more tolerant Romans didn't like the idea of a fortified temple on this high mountainside.

As a child, Rachel learned God's Law as teachers taught the Torah in the local synagogue just outside the village.[45] Dressed in white, she blended in with similarly dressed worshippers, young and old, streaming to the synagogue. Their synagogue, as did all Samaritan synagogues, faced Mount Gerizim, unlike the Jewish forgeries in Israel and

---

Shechem. It forms the south side of the valley, with the north side formed by Mount Ebal. Gerizim is one of the highest peaks west of the Jordan, about 881 m (2,890 ft) above sea level. Mount Ebal is 59 m (193 ft) higher.

[42] Shechem is about 30 mi (49 km) north of Jerusalem.

[43] See Deuteronomy 11:29.

[44] The Samaritan temple was destroyed by John Hyrcanus about 126 BC.

[45] Samaritans built their synagogues outside their villages and cities, whereas Jewish Synagogues were usually central to their neighborhood. Jews worshipped in Jerusalem and learned in their synagogues. Along with Mt. Gerizim, the Samaritans worshipped in their synagogues, so they believed these should be "outside the camp" due to Exodus 33:7.

abroad.[46] Though Rachel didn't know exactly what the Jews altered, she heard the Jewish Torah was different from theirs and that the Jews had added many volumes to their sacred book.[47] Prayers and singing accompanied Torah readings. At least, the synagogue was nearby; during Passover and other major pilgrimages, worship meant climbing Mount Gerizim to gather at its sacred summit.

Apart from religious matters, Rachel's mother taught her how to be a good wife. Cooking, sewing and seemingly endless cleaning filled her days. From her earliest memories she had learned to fetch water from Jacob's well[48],

---

[46] Jewish synagogues faced Jerusalem.

[47] The Samaritans rejected all but the first five books of the Law (Genesis, Exodus, Leviticus, Numbers, and Deuteronomy) as the other prophets and books clearly confirmed Jerusalem as the city God chose for His temple. The Samaritans also made slight adjustments to the books of the Law to better establish worship at Mount Gerizim.

[48] Jacob's well, or the Well of Sychar, is a 41 meter (135 ft) deep rock hewn well, about 7½ ft in diameter below a narrower neck, associated with Jacob for over two millennia. While not mentioned in the Old Testament, Jacob camped near Shechem in Genesis 33:18-20. The well is believed to be on the land he purchased at that time. Jewish, Samaritan, Christian and even later Muslim traditions all associate this still existing well with Jacob.

first accompanying her mother. Soon her mother assigned Rachel that daily responsibility as a *very* young woman. The clay pot, filled with water, was heavy on her shoulder on the way home. It was not only necessary to draw water for home use. On arrival, Rachel had to first provide water for their animals which dutifully followed her to the well. At least at the well, she could visit with other girls her own age. Better still, she could sometimes discretely consider some of the young men who occasionally came out specifically to see the young women.[49] The well was the only place boys could observe these young ladies away from the watchful eyes of the girl's male relatives. She dreamed that her future husband would be as handsome as some of those she saw.

Rachel's parents arranged her betrothal while she was still a very young woman. They later granted permission for the marriage to take place when she was thirteen years-old, her husband was five years older.[50] He unquestionably wasn't what she had dreamed about. About a year into the marriage, she decided she could find better and returned to her parent's home. The scorn of being a young divorcee bothered her a bit.

The next seven years were a blur. The divorces weren't always of her choice, but either way they happened. Four more husbands and again Rachel was unmarried. Her dream of finding a perfect husband had long since faded. She was almost immune to the contempt respectable families showed her almost daily. And, following this last divorce, now her father refused to allow her to return home.

---

[49] In Old Testament times, the local well was where Isaac's wife Rebecca was found (Genesis 24:10-28), later Jacob meets Rachel (Genesis 29:1-11), and even Moses meets his future bride Zipporah (Exodus 2:15-22). Saul met some young women there while searching for his father's donkeys (1 Samuel 9:3-12).

[50] Jewish Rabbi's authorized the marriage of a young woman at 12 years plus 1 day. Samaritan practice was similar.

Her latest man provided a roof over her head. Rachel's scandalous behavior no longer shocked anyone; she had functionally become what they had long considered her: a harlot. In her mind, why bother to marry anyway? It never lasted. Rachel found it easy to blame God for everything. Whether it be festivals, synagogue, or even going to the well, she was no longer welcome in polite society. Her wishful thoughts and search for pleasure had brought her to this.

Most women of Sychar fetched water from the well in the early evening, some in the early morning. Rachel went at midday because *they* wouldn't be there. The days of meeting friends at the well were long past; she had no friends. On this day as Rachel approached the well, it surprised her to see a stranger, a man, sitting there. His accent betrayed him as Jew, a Galilean no less.[51] Even knowing she was a Samaritan, and obviously an outcast by her untimely and solitary arrival, this man asked her for a drink of water. His asking shocked her. Samaritans and Jews never helped the other.

Rachel met Jesus. She drank of the living water that Jesus freely offered.[52] He knew her past in detail; he knew she was now living with a man unmarried. He made clear the true

---

[51] Galileans had a distinctive accent over even Judean Jews. See Matthew 26:69 & 73.

[52] This woman's entire encounter with Jesus is recorded in John 4:3-42

word of God leading to salvation had belonged to the Jews. Through Jesus' words she came to understand that worship of God must be in spirit and in truth, not just in the right place. She believed He was the promised Messiah.

It stunned Jesus' disciples that He was speaking with *this* woman as they returned. They were still trying to figure out why Jesus had brought them this way at all. The proper way to travel from Galilee to Judah was to avoid all Samaritan territory. They had already suffered scorn from locals while trying to buy food.

Rachel hardly noticed the disciple's shocked looks. She now wanted to share Jesus with everyone in Sychar. In her excitement, she forgot what everyone thought about her, she quickly ran into town telling everyone about Him. Soon a crowd headed to Jacob's well. While some believed her, many more came out of curiosity, or perhaps hoping to prove her insane. Regardless of why they came, many more believed in Jesus after hearing Him speak.

Jesus and his disciples, these Jews, stayed in Samaritan Sychar for two days. All these believing followers of Jesus were willing to accept one another including the now repentant serial-divorcee Rachel. Would you?

## Paula of Rome

Paula grew up in Rome. The empire had seen major changes since its inception. Only a few decades before her birth[53] Constantine, a former general, declared himself *Augustus* and was supported by his troops from Gaul.[54] As self-proclaimed

---

[53] Paula was born in Rome in 347 AD.

[54] Gaul was a region of Western Europe encompassing Gallia Celtica (Switzerland, most of France, Luxembourg, and Germany west of the Rhine), Gallia Belgica (Belgium, Netherlands, and northern

emperor he marched on Rome and defeated the former emperor Maxentius. Some said Constantine received a vision telling him *In Hoc Signo Vinces*, with this sign you shall win.[55] The sign he claimed to see was the Chi-Rho[56] symbol which represented the first two letters of *Cristos* or Christ. His army conquered Rome bearing this symbol on their *vexillum*,[57] something unique as Roman armies had only ever used the standards of Roman gods and rulers

before.[58] Yes, over the last three centuries Christians had spread throughout the empire, but – at best – officials tolerated them. Often superficial toleration turned to open or encouraged persecution. But now Constantine claimed the name of Christ.

It's not as if Constantine had been a Christian before his vision. Even after he took office in Rome, he didn't act

---

Germany), and Gallia Aquitania (Southwest France).

[55] Recorded shortly afterward by the historian Eusebius of Caesarea who lived from 263-339 AD.

[56] The Chi-Rho is an early form of a christogram, created by superimposing the first two letters—chi (X) and rho (P) —of the Greek word XPIΣTOΣ (*Khristos*) in such a way that the vertical stroke of the rho intersects the center of the chi.

[57] A *vexillum* (plural *vexilla*) was a flag-like or banner object used as a military standard. It was often carried on a pole or spear.

[58] Constantine took Rome in 312 AD.

much like a Christian. Murdering his wife Fausta by boiling her alive and executing his son Crispus was distinctly unchristian.[59] Even his new capital city of Byzantium, now renamed Constantinople[60], had remaining pagan temples. Constantine allowed the pagans to continue their rituals provided they didn't force Christian participation. While the emperor personally stopped attending rituals at the pagan temples, it wasn't until his deathbed that he asked for a Christian baptism.[61]

Constantine's formal toleration and increasing encouragement of Christianity – some would even say favoritism towards Christianity – allowed Christians to now publicly serve in government.

Unsurprisingly, most of Rome's prominent families declared their conversion to Christianity. The empire's later division following Constantine's death brought much insecurity and instability to the empire. Yet, somehow, Rome's wealthy and connected always managed to thrive despite these top-level changes and governmental problems.

---

[59] In 326 AD, Constantine ordered a court to convict his son and have him executed by hanging. A few months later Constantine had his wife and mother of his deceased son killed in an overheated bath.

[60] Constantine founded Constantinople in 326 AD.

[61] Constantine was baptized by Eusebius, the bishop of Nicomedia, in 337 AD – the year of his death.

In a city where connections and heredity meant everything, Paula's birth was to the right family. Her lineage gave her the best of connections as a member of Rome's noble Gracchi[62] and Scipios[63] families.

Her parents, of course, wanted Paula to continue this legacy, so they sought a betrothal that would strengthen her pedigree and give them extra connections too. They were successful in making such an arrangement, with Toxotius now her promised husband. His lineage was ancient Æneas bloodline and of the powerful Julii.[64] They couldn't have done better.

---

[62] The Gracchi are descendants of the Gracchi brothers, Tiberius and Gaius, famous plebian tribunes between 133 and 121 BC. They worked to distribute public lands normally controlled by Roman aristocrats to the urban poor and army veterans. Both were ultimately assassinated. First, the senate's conservative faction had Tiberius and 300 of his supporters clubbed to death (with some senators personally participating). Ten years later, as the Gracchi reforms continued, the same faction raised a mob to silence the remaining brother. They forced Gaius to commit suicide and then arrested three thousand of his followers who were all likewise executed.

[63] The Scipios were descendants of Publius Cornelius Scipio, who died in 211 BC. A Roman Republic general and statesman, his son Scipio Africanus became legendary as a Roman general and consul. He was considered the greatest military strategist in Roman history, defeating Hannibal at the final battle of Zama, in Tunisia, in 202 BC.

[64] Æneas was a legendary Greco-Roman character that Caesar Augustus tied into Rome's traditional founding legend of Romulus

It didn't hurt when troops proclaimed Flavius Claudius Julianus, or Julian, also of the Julii, as Augustus and Caesar of the western empire. To everyone's surprise, five years later Julian became emperor of an again unified Empire, east and west.[65] Julian was different. At age twenty, he had left the way of Christianity and studied the pagan gods. Two years later he traveled to Athens resulting in his initiation into the Eleusinian Mysteries.[66] From that time onward he sought to restore these pagan gods to their rightful place. Having won

---

and Remus. The gens Julia were perhaps the most ancient patrician family in Rome. Its members attained the highest dignities of state during the Roman Republic. The later founding of the Empire rested in this family, namely dictator Gaius Julius Caesar, the grand uncle of the emperor Augustus, through whom the name was passed to the first century's Julio-Claudian dynasty.

[65] Julian, later known as Julian the Apostate, became emperor of the entire Empire in 361 AD.

[66] The Eleusinian Mysteries were annual admissions for the secrecy shrouded cult of Demeter and Persephone based in Eleusis, Greece.

the Emperor's office, Julian was now in position to make these changes.

Soon, pagan temples were again thriving in Rome and Constantinople. Julian knew better than to openly attack Christianity. He didn't ban Christian churches, he merely removed their authority and encouraged divisive Christian sects, giving every schism equal standing.

To demolish the Christianity he so despised, Julian encouraged strife in the church. He welcomed hostile teachers and encouraged the return of banished heretics with a goal of constant church conflict and division. Further, Julian banned Christian schools, mandating all Christian children attend the state's new and well-funded pagan schools. Publication and state circulation of *Adversus Christianos*, a written work in opposition to Christianity soon followed. This well-crafted literary work directly attacked the doctrine of Christ.

While Julian didn't openly encourage persecution of Christians, unavoidable clashes followed. The state mostly ignored this violence and ruled favorably for the pagans in court. In contrast, the slightest offense by a Christian resulted in swift and harsh punishment.

The Julii quickly abandoned Christianity and embraced the paganism of their new emperor, thus ensuring they would preserve their longstanding positions of power. Paula wondered if this change would affect her betrothal now that Toxotius was a pagan. In the end, it didn't matter. She and her family quietly remained Christians and yet her parents

encouraged her to still marry him. Her father felt connections in both factions were desirable. So, with her consent, Toxotius' family arranged his wedding to Paula a year later as she turned 15.[67]

Paula's life was everything she had dreamt of. Her status and luxurious circumstances provided her an envious way of life. And she readily displayed her wealth and status by dressing in silks and having personal slaves carry her about the city.[68]

Children soon followed her marriage, with the birth of Blaesilla, Paulina, Eustochium, and Rufina – all daughters. Finally, she had a son, named Toxotius after his father. While some might have found it stressful raising five young children, Paula had slaves to help with this.

---

[67] "In her mid-teens, Paula was married to the nobleman Toxotius" – Jerome. This would've been about 362 AD. My primary source for specific details of Paula's life come from Jerome, Letter 108, *To Eustochium*.

[68] The slaves tasked with accompanying Paula were all eunuchs.

Emperor Julian's revival of paganism faltered with his death in 363 AD. His short-lived successor, Jovian, rolled back his "reforms" and restored Christianity as the state religion.[69]

Unsurprisingly, most of the Julii again publicly embraced Christianity.[70] Paula attended church with her children, her husband sometimes now accompanying though he still privately expressed sentiments favoring the pagan gods over Christ.

Life was good. With status, great food, the latest fashions, social connections,

---

[69] Jovian ruled for less than eight months before dying from battle wounds. He selected Valentinian as his heir. Valentinian makes his brother Valens eastern emperor and takes the west for himself. The result was a permanent separation of the empire.

[70] Especially in 380 AD when successor emperor Theodosius the Great issued the Edict of Thessalonica making Christianity the sole and official religion of the empire.

family, hardworking slaves, and a wonderful husband, Paula couldn't have asked for more.

And then, her world came crashing to the ground. At age 32, Paula was a widow.[71] The death of Toxotius devastated her. She couldn't imagine life without him. In her mourning, she wished she too was dead and, indeed, almost died. Yet, in her grief, she providentially met Marcella.

Marcella was a widow,[72] similarly a Christian from a noble family, living in a palace on Aventine Hill.[73] Yet she was different. Marcella lived her Christianity and her friends knew she held fast to Christ. Hers wasn't a superficial Christianity like the kind easily cast aside by the Julii. It was at her house that Paula heard fervent prayer and saw a noble woman actively helping Rome's ever-present poor. Marcella chose "to store her money in the stomachs of the poor rather than to keep it at her own disposal." She

was passionate about God's Word and remained firm in it even as many heresies found their way to Rome. Several recalled her singing...

---

[71] Toxotius died in 379 AD.

[72] Having been married for a mere 7 months.

[73] My primary source for specific details of Marcella's life come from Jerome, Letter 127, *To Principia*.

"Your words have I hid in mine heart that I might not sin against you."[74]

At Marcella's urging, Paula provided lodging for a pastor, Epiphanius of Salamis, coming to Rome for a conference. While staying elsewhere, Epiphanius' friend Paulinus of Antioch was also a frequent guest for meals. She enjoyed many deep spiritual conversations with these godly men. It was Epiphanius and Paulinus who introduced Paula to Jerome,[75] soon becoming another dear friend.

As Paula learned God's word she grew in faith and she hungered to know more. Her faith in Jesus Christ changed her outlook, giving her hope. Gone were her days focused on luxury and indifference. Like Marcella, she became known as someone actively helping the sick and poor in Jesus' name.

Paula's growing faith carried her through trials of the next few years including the death of her daughter Blaesilla's husband and then Blaesilla's death in the same year. Her son was also a source of grief, as he followed his father's example and that of the Julii – rejecting Christianity and embracing paganism. Toxotius even married the daughter of the pagan priest Albinus, a betrothal arranged while his father was still alive. Yet, she never stopped praying for him and God blessed her to see him later come to faith.

Paula welcomed every moment she had while learning from Jerome. His knowledge of Scripture was vast. He had firsthand knowledge of the Bible lands and read God's Word in its original languages. Jerome longed to return to Palestine, so the day came all too soon when Paula and Marcella tearfully bid him good-bye.[76]

---

[74] A song reflecting Psalms 119:11.

[75] Jerome was almost the same age as Paula, being born in 348 AD.

[76] In May of 385, Jerome set sail for Syrian Antioch.

A few months later Paula decided that she also needed to see the lands of the Bible. So, with her daughter Eustochium, she set sail.

Stopping at Cyprus, Epiphanius welcomed her to the island. And as she visited the area's churches, she generously helped as many as she could. Meeting with Jerome in Antioch, he became Paula's guide as they visited Tyre & Sidon, followed by the lands of ancient Israel. Not only did she learn of a multitude of Biblical locales, Paula continued to aid people physically in every community she visited. Finally, they also toured Egypt to visit the land of Jesus' childhood and the Old

Testament patriarchs.

In Egypt, Paula determined to not return to Rome but rather to move to Bethlehem. She now wanted permanently to remain in the land of her Savior's birth. In Bethlehem, at her expense, she built a guesthouse for those in need and traveling. This included separate living quarters for men and women wishing to come and study and serve.[77]

Her passion to study scripture continued unabated and she persuaded Jerome to read aloud to her the entire Bible in its original languages.[78]

---

[77] Paula was over the women's residence and Jerome the men.

[78] Jerome said of Paul's insistence: "She compelled me."

In her continued studies, she now learned those original languages and, when finding a lack of commentaries on many Bible books, she prodded and compelled Jerome to begin this labor. As Jerome needed rare manuscripts and reference books, Paula bought these for him at her own

expense. Her efforts finally led to him completing a Latin translation of the Bible from the original languages. Paula and her daughter then copied Jerome's manuscripts for circulation.

Paula wasn't merely a passive observer of Jerome's translation efforts. Rather, she was an invaluable partner. As she had promised in his reluctantly agreeing to start this task,[79] Paula provided criticism, advice and encouragement. Her duties included regularly proofing and editing his manuscripts and using her newfound fluency in the original languages to aid in translation word choices.

Paula of Rome, as most knew her in Palestine, never returned to her former life. She poured out her life and finances for the sake of Christ's kingdom.[80]

---

[79] Jerome was overwhelmed at the idea of taking on this task, understanding the long-term importance of its accuracy.

[80] Jerome wrote of Paula in 404 AD, the year of her death: "Jesus is witness that Paula las left not a single penny to her daughter." That same year, Paula the Younger, came to join Eustochium in Bethlehem. She was the daughter of Paula's once pagan son,

Would you befriend this formerly religiously indifferent aristocrat and slave owner, once focused on luxury at the expense of others?

Would you join with Christ's church and use the Latin Vulgate Bible that she labored to help Jerome create, as did most of the western church over a thousand years?[81]

---

Toxotius, now also a believer. She too became Jerome's friend and, at his death in 420 AD, was present to "close his eyes."

[81] Paula almost lived to see Jerome's Latin Vulgate complete. He published it in 405 shortly after she died in 404. Jerome addresses her daughter in his great work's preface: "Now that the blessed and venerable Paula has slept in the Lord, I have not been able to refuse you, Eustochium, virgin of Christ, these books which I promised to your mother."

# Chapter Five

## Tax Collectors and Extortionists

### Levi

Levi grew up in Herodian Galilee in the early first century. Perhaps Roman occupied Galilee would be better wording. Herod Antipas ruled only because the Roman Emperor granted him this power, even as they had done for His father before him. Herod had no problem using Roman auxiliary troops to enforce his laws. Levi's father Alphaeus[82] named him after one of Israel's patriarchs, the third son of Jacob.[83] His parents had him circumcised on the eighth day and taught him about God's law. He attended his people's annual great festivals in God's holy city of Jerusalem and offered the Law's prescribed sacrifices.

Work was scarce in Galilee – at least well-paying work. What was more important? He could remain poor and in harmony with other Jews or he could work for Herod and live a life of relative luxury. Levi chose the latter.

---

[82] See Mark 2:13.

[83] See Genesis 29:34.

One of King Herod's principal revenue sources, granted him by the Romans, was to tax people and goods entering or leaving his territory. Of course, Rome exempted its

citizens from any customs tax, but there were few citizens in this region. Otherwise, everyone coming and going, even from the nearby Israeli Galilean province of Herod's brother Phillip or Rome-ruled Judah, were fair game. Levi was confident that he could make good money from this enterprise; all he had to do was, perhaps, be a little overzealous. Herod, in standard fashion, had put the office of border-tax collector up for auction. Levi only needed to estimate what he thought he could collect and bid less than that. Of course, only the potential tax collector bidding the highest would get the coveted job. So, like those before him, he reluctantly bid what he considered top dollar and worked on the assumption he'd find a way to collect even more during the term of his lease.

Extracting more than their fair share of tax revenue was a high-stake game for their entire profession. The *publicani's* corrupt and unethical methods were the problem. These tax collectors regularly drew the ire of the Pharisees exercising their zealousness for God's law. Plus, everyone despised anyone willing to work with Herod, himself a compromiser who did little to hide his affection for Greco-Roman traditions over true Jewish piety. All these charges against the *publicani* gained them a longstanding reputation synonymous with sinners.[84] For Levi, the increased income was

---

[84] Mark 2:15  And as Jesus reclined at table in his house, many tax collectors and sinners were reclining with Jesus and his disciples, for

worth the maligned reputation – there was a good chance he could get rich. This thought pleased him greatly. And weren't riches a sign of God's blessing and favor?

Levi's bid didn't win the *publicani* auction; he should have bid higher. Since he knew the person who won, he figured a piece of the pie was better than nothing. For now, he would settle for being an ordinary tax collector working for the chief *publicani*. At least he could make decent wages if he met his tax-collecting quotas. It helped that Levi worked on the main road between Herod's territory and the region controlled by Herod's brother Philip. Specifically, this was the main road leaving Capernaum going east to Bethsaida.[85] This well-traveled trade route also led north to Caesarea Philippi and south on the eastern side of Galilee to the mostly Gentile Decapolis cities.[86] If you were crossing the Jordan River headed west, you were going to have an appointment with Levi or one of his associate tax collectors. Here they could also capitalize on Pharisaical traditions. Those excessively righteous teachers wouldn't allow anyone to carry even a piece of paper

---

there were many who followed him. [16] And the scribes of the Pharisees, when they saw that he was eating with sinners and tax collectors, said to his disciples, "Why does he eat with tax collectors and sinners?" [17] And when Jesus heard it, he said to them, "Those who are well have no need of a physician, but those who are sick. I came not to call the righteous, but sinners."

[85] This was near the Sea of Galilee at Capernaum (compare Mark 2:1 and Mark 2:13) – the edge of Herod Antipas' territory where the Jordan enters the northern tip of sea.

[86] The Decapolis was a group of ten cities all located east of the Jordan River except Scythopolis which was southwest of Galilee. The cities acted as a group because of their language, culture, location, and political status. Each were relatively wealthy autonomous city-states dependent on Rome.

on Shabbat,[87] claiming it was "work". So, any diligent tax collector could easily double tax anyone having to pass the border twice on that day as they couldn't carry their receipt. Levi had no problem working on Shabbat. Why miss the revenue from traveling Gentiles and the possible double taxing of Jews making shorter trips to the nearby synagogue in Capernaum? Did they think he would remember what they were carrying on their way in? Besides, what's the worst other Jews could call him? A "tax collector?"

In fact, Levi mostly didn't even go by his Hebrew name, choosing to use his Aramaic name instead. Matthaios, or Matthew, was easier to pronounce in Greek and this was the Roman world's business language. And, these days, Matthew mostly spent his time accepting Gentiles if he wasn't with other tax collectors.

Then Levi met Jesus – literally. He had heard a few stories about this teacher and that He was far different from the Pharisees. And now, this man – different from anyone he had ever met before – stopped, looked him in the eye and said, "Follow me!" And Matthew did, abandoning his tax booth, and his life was never the same.[88] Jesus was even willing to eat with Matthew's other tax collector friends.[89] As one of Jesus' twelve apostles, Matthew saw all that happened during Jesus' ministry and witnessed His death on the cross. And he was present when Jesus appeared resurrected and later when Jesus rose into heaven. He followed Jesus and he had no doubt that this was the promised Messiah of the Jews. God later had Matthew write the key events of this period in his gospel for his fellow Jews. For decades he traveled widely even beyond the Roman Empire to share the good news with the Persians

---

[87] Shabbat is the weekly Sabbath beginning at sundown on Friday and ending at sundown on Saturday. The Mosaic law mandated no work on this day; see Exodus 20:8-11.

[88] See Matthew 9:9, Mark 2:13-14, and Luke 5:27-28.

[89] See Luke 5:29-32 and Matthew 9:10-13.

and the Parthians.[90] In fellowship with believers, both Jews and Gentiles, he served the Lord until his death. Would you befriend this reformed and transformed tax collector?

## Zacchaeus

Zacchaeus was all Levi once was and worse. Zacchaeus' name in Hebrew meant "innocent," a now ironically laughable idea to other Jews. This man was worse than Levi in that he worked directly for the Roman government. This meant he worked for the detestable Pontius Pilatus, who ruled over Judea from Caesarea Maritima. He was the fifth and latest prefect, or governor, since the Emperor deposed Herod Archelaus thirteen years earlier. Zacchaeus also had bid on the opportunity to collect taxes. Except here, every denarius[91] he paid would go straight into Caesar's treasury.

Zacchaeus was the big man, of small stature, [92] in Jericho. If Levi thought this was a good opportunity in backwoods Galilee, it paled in comparison to the traffic coming into Judea at Jericho. Here all travelers from Arabia, or Syria, had to pass through his collection point. Even those coming from faraway Persia would have come via this route. And, as always, you could tax them coming and going. This was the main road for all Jews coming to Jerusalem for the annual mandated festivals. Zacchaeus had heard the long-told story of a tax collector who collected taxes from eastern magi

---

[90] The Persians and Parthians included people in the regions now known as Iraq and Iran. During the Assyrian and Babylonian eras, many Jews were resettled in this region.

[91] A denarius was a common Roman coin equivalent to a day's pay for a laborer.

[92] "He was of little stature" (Luke 19:3)

coming to Jerusalem with expensive gifts.[93] He dreamed of such a windfall.

You couldn't find a better spot for a tax collector, except perhaps at the capital city seaport of Caesarea Maritima. Of course, a high traffic location such as Jericho needed much help. Zacchaeus was holder of the Roman contract, the chief *publicani* over all other tax collectors at Jericho.[94] All the other tax collectors answered to him. It was worth his efforts managing all this, as it meant Zacchaeus profited most, proven by how rich he had become through his collaboration with Rome.[95]

Zacchaeus met Jesus while using a vantage point in an easily climbed sycamore to catch a glimpse of the teacher as he passed through the city. In fact, Jesus invited himself into Zacchaeus' home. Not only did Zacchaeus welcome Jesus into his house that day, he also became a believer in Jesus Christ. This didn't mean abandoning his job; it gave Zacchaeus the opportunity to show that he was a changed man.[96] Now, regardless of the personal cost, he was going to be something perhaps never seen in the Roman world before. Zacchaeus had become an honest tax collector and a welcoming stop for believers on their way to Jerusalem.[97]

---

[93] This happened shortly after Jesus' birth; see Matthew 2:1 & 11.

[94] "Chief among the publicans" (Luke 19:2)

[95] "He was rich" (Luke 19:3).

[96] Rome was the governing power, so working for Rome was legitimate work no matter how poorly other Jews thought of it. See Romans 13:1.

[97] Zacchaeus' full story is found in Luke 19:1-10.

Shortly after Jesus' visit, Zacchaeus also went to Jerusalem for the Passover as the Law demanded of all Jewish males.[98] There he soon learned the Romans had crucified Jesus. His walk back to Jericho seemed longer than normal. To his amazement, another traveler from Jerusalem a few days later

spread the news of reports that Jesus was alive, risen from the grave! And he believed. This was the man Zacchaeus would forever follow.

Jesus and his disciples didn't shun former or continuing tax collectors who had come to faith in Jesus such as Levi and Zacchaeus. These vile thieving traitors – detestable sinners – became brothers in the Lord, saints struggling to no longer sin.

How about you? Knowing their past, would you eat with these men?

---

[98] See Exodus 23:14-17 and Leviticus 23:4-8

# Chapter Six

## A Crazy Demoniac and Powerful Pagan

### Mary Magdalene

Home for Mary was a thriving center of commerce on the western coastline of the Sea of Galilee. Had Herod Antipas not built Tiberias further south on the seacoast a few years earlier, this would have been the largest urban center on the

western side of the Sea.[99]

Boat building and fish salting were the backbone of Magdala's economy. The dock area was always busy. Mary was oblivious to the sea's beauty to her east. Her focus and fascination were the great cliffs of the Arbel towering over the town to the west. It was there centuries earlier that a ruler killed women and children, hurling them from the heights of these cliffs.[100] Further, in the past century, Herod the Great had burned out rebels that had hidden on this mountainside. He too slaughtered men, women and children also casting them down from this mountain precipice.[101] It was fitting that the low foothill between the cliffs and town had become Magdala's local graveyard. All this death and devastation held Mary spellbound.

Mary's parents had made sure she attended Synagogue on the north side of town, both for her education and to hear the Law's reading on the weekly Shabbat. Both her parents tended to the family business and obviously they had been quite successful, as she knew they were better off than many in town. Of course, they wanted her to marry a good Jewish boy and had arranged her betrothal to a respectable family.

Her parents' plans and dreams aside, everything changed seemingly overnight. Their death, the voices she started hearing in her head, and her wild behavioral shifts turned Mary into a different person. Her betrothed and his

---

[99] Scholars variously date Tiberias' founding from 18 to 20 AD (the first coins featuring the city appearing in 20 AD). Herod Antipas made the new city his capital, and named the city after the Roman emperor, Tiberius Caesar.

[100] Hosea 10:14b ... as Shalman destroyed Beth-arbel on the day of battle; mothers were dashed in pieces with their children.

[101] See Josephus, Wars of the Jews, 1.16.4-5

family no longer wanted to have anything to do with her and they quickly ended the relationship. While Mary had money and resources, they meant nothing to her as her life spiraled out of control. Unsurprisingly, everyone ostracized her. Mary was the most common name an Israeli girl could have; most people easily knew two or three. Regardless, everyone around western Galilee knew of *this* Mary and nobody wanted to be around this crazy person.

Mary heard about a man called Jesus, first overhearing some travelers from Capernaum. They claimed he ate with tax collectors and sinners.[102]
He supposedly could heal the sick. Even with everyone avoiding her, Mary later heard talk that he had raised a man from the dead in a village in southwestern Galilee.[103] While others seemed enthralled with Him, hoping He was the promised Messiah, she had an inexplicable hatred for the man. The voices in her head said He needed to die.[104]

Mary often spent time outside Magdala, in more desolate places, where she was less likely to run into people. To

---

[102] See Luke 5:29-32.

[103] See Luke 7:11-17.

[104] The Bible often associates fascination with death with demon possession: see Matthew 8:28; Mark 5:2-5; and Luke 8:27. Satan certainly wanted to see Jesus dead; see 1 Corinthians 2:8, John 10:10, and Luke 22:3.

her surprise, it was there she met Jesus.[105] Every voice in her head screamed at her to hate him and to harm him. But at that moment Jesus spoke to the demons that had long controlled her. He ordered them to forever leave her and she was instantly free. And Jesus forgave her sins. Mary knew, then and there, that she had found God's promised Messiah. From that moment onward she would follow no one else. She now had a purpose for all the possessions she had previously despised and squandered. With no reason to stay in Magdala, Mary now traveled with Jesus using her money to help support His ministry.[106]

Jesus' disciples quickly named her Mary Magdalene, after her hometown, to set her apart from all the other women they knew who shared her name.

Mary followed Jesus even on His final journey to Jerusalem and witnessed His crucifixion.[107] Better yet, she was the first one to find the tomb empty, with its huge stone rolled away, three days later, before dawn on Sunday morning. After seeing his brutal death, to her amazement, Jesus showed himself to her alive![108]

---

[105] Jesus often spent time in desolate places; see Luke 5:16.

[106] See Luke 8:1-3. That Mary is listed first implies she was most important of those listed, perhaps playing the greatest role in this support.

[107] See John 19:25, Mark 15:40, and Matthew 27:55-56.

[108] See John 20:1, 11-17.

For many months, Jesus and his disciples openly and unashamedly traveled with this formerly demon-controlled woman. In fact, of everyone Jesus could have first shown Himself to after He rose from the grave, He chose Mary.[109] Would you be willing to appear with this woman or accept her generous support?

## Ka'ahumanu

Ka'ahumanu's birth was in a cave on the Hawaiian island of Maui in 1768. Her father was a fugitive, hiding from the ruling authorities on the island of Hawai'i. To be fair, the man he fled from was openly killing any chief standing in his way, even erecting a house of bones from his enemies' skeletons. In time, circumstances improved for Ka'ahumanu as her father became the royal governor of Maui under the ruler Kamehameha.

Ka'ahumanu's father soon arranged her marriage to king Kamehameha. At age thirteen she welcomed this marriage and quickly endeared herself to the king, becoming his favorite of his many wives. She encouraged his war to subdue and unify all the islands. Unquestionably, Ka'ahumanu was the most powerful of the king's wives and she enjoyed this power. When the king unexpectedly died, she publicly declared it had been his wish that she become co-ruler with her son Liholiho, then 22 years old.[110] She successfully held onto power, growing her power base. Even when Liholiho unexpectedly died, she remained queen regent during the later reign of his half-brother.[111]

---

[109] See John 20:18.

[110] Liholiho took the name Kamehameha II, his rule beginning in 1819.

[111] He assumed the throne in 1825 under the name Kamehameha III

As a child Ka'ahumanu's parent taught her about the many gods they worshiped, including the volcano deity Pele.[112] She understood that besides the major gods, there were lesser

personal and family guardian gods, or *'aumakua*, and those considered the deified dead. She sought wisdom from these gods through dreams, images, and nature. The priests, or *kahuna*, of course, were specialists in the rituals and techniques essential in contacting the gods. Religion controlled everyone's life regardless of their rank or position in society. Dissatisfied gods sent drought and disease.

The king and his queens, including Ka'ahumanu, relied

---

though his full royal name was Keaweawe'ula Kīwala'ō Kauikeaouli Kaleiopapa Kalani Waiakua Kalanikau Iokikilo Kīwala'ō i ke kapu Kamehameha.

[112] Pele is the goddess of volcanoes and fire and considered creator of the Hawaiian Islands. She is also called *Pele-honua-mea*, or "Pele of the sacred land," the one who shaped the sacred land.

66

on the *kahuna nui*, the high priest, on how to win divine support. Ironically, people considered Ka'ahumanu an earthly goddess. She especially worshiped and sought help from Haumea, the goddess of fertility and mother of Pele, plus the water-spirit goddess Kihawahine. Human sacrifice was sometimes necessary to appease the highest Kū gods and only a major chief could offer these burned human sacrifices to pray for the king or queen regent's health and national prosperity. Slaves, war captives, and *kapu*-breakers (anyone who broke religious and societal taboos) were candidates for such

sacrifices.

Ka'ahumanu hoped that enough ritual and her personal god would keep her soul from *Milu*, the underworld. Worse still, anyone without a personal god could become a forlorn spirit cursed to wander the earth. The death of her husband, the king, caused Ka'ahumanu to think a lot about death.[113] Religious rituals and gods that couldn't prevent the death of this powerful husband and father disillusioned the queen and her co-regent son.

---

[113] Kamehameha I died in May 1819.

Only a few months later, Protestant Christian missionaries arrived on the island from Boston. [114]

Ka'ahumanu was ready to hear the message these missionaries brought and befriended Hiram and Sybil Bingham. For the first time, the queen heard about the one true creator God and His son's once-for-all sacrifice on the cross.[115] It wasn't long before Ka'ahumanu placed her faith in Jesus, who had proven He had triumphed over death by rising from the grave.[116] She soon obeyed her Lord's command for baptism, with her subjects publicly witnessing this on December 5, 1825.

Ka'ahumanu used the rest of her rule to help spread the message of Jesus to her people, encouraging them to follow her example and turn to Christ. This included setting up laws based on Biblical values. She lived to see work completed in translating a major portion of the *Baibala*, the Bible, into the Hawaiian language. The publishers presented the first completed copy of the New Testament to her as she fell ill in 1827. She treasured this and kept it with her until her death on

---

[114] These first missionaries to Hawaii arrived on a ship called the Thaddeus, arriving on March 30, 1820. They included the couple Hiram and Sybil Bingham, plus Asa and Lucy Thurston. More arrived in 1822, including the first British missionary William Ellis.

[115] See Hebrews 7:27 and Romans 6:5-10.

[116] Ka'ahumanu publicly announced her conversion to Christianity in April of 1824.

June 5, 1832.[117]

Queen Ka'ahumanu's funeral took place in the Kawaiahaʻo Church that she had commissioned at the site of her baptism.[118] From her time until the present, many believers have been willing to identify with this repentant pagan formerly with blood on her hands. Would you?

---

[117] The entire Bible, the *Palapala Hemolele*, with *Buke I* (the Old Testament) and *Buke II* (the New Testament) was published after her death, from 1837 to 1839.

[118] The Kawaiahaʻo Church still stands at this site.

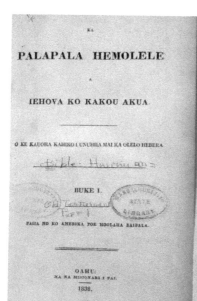

K4

# PALAPALA HEMOLELE

A

## IEHOVA KO KAKOU AKUA.

O KE KAUOHA KAHIKO I UNUHIIA MAI KA OLELO HEBERA

BUKE 1.

PAIIA NO KO AMERIKA POE HOOLAHA BAIBALA.

OAHU:
NA NA MISIONARI I PAI.
1838.

Ka Moolelo Kinohi, i kakauia'i e Mose.

MOKUNA I.

No ka he Akua hana ana i ka lani a me ka honua, ia kamaka a me na hihiolean.

1 KINOHI hana ke Akua i ka lani a me ka honua.

2 He ano ole ka honua, ua olohelohe; a maluna no o ka hohonu ka poeli. Hoopunana iho la ka Uhane o ke Akua maluna o ka wai.

3 I iho la ke Akua, I malamalama; a ua malamalama ae la.

4 Nana ae la ke Akua i ka malamalama, Ua maikai; a hookaawale ae la ke Akua mawaena o ka malamalama, a me ka pouli.

5 Kapa mai la ke Akua i ka malamalama, he Ao, a kapa mai hoi ia i ka pouli, he Po. A o ke ahiahi a me ke kakahiaka, o ka la mua ia.

6 I iho la ke Akua, I aouli mawaena o na wai, i mea hookaawale i kekahi wai me kekahi wai.

7 Hana iho la ke Akua i ke aouli; a hookaawale ae la ia i ka wai malalo o ke aouli, me ka wai maluna o ke aouli: a pela io no.

8 Kapa iho la ke Akua i ke aouli, he Lani. A o ke ahiahi a me ke kakahiaka, o ka lua ia o ka la.

9 I iho la ke Akua, E hui pu na wai malalo o ka lani i kahi hookahi, i ikea ai kahi maloo: a pela io no.

10 Kapa iho la ke Akua i kahi maloo, he Aina, a kapa iho la oia i na wai i hui pu ia'i, o na moana: a nana ae la ke Akua, ua maikai.

11 I iho la ke Akua, E hoouliu mai ka honua i ka mauu, a me ka launahele e hua ana i ka hua ma kona ano iho, a me ka laau, e hua ana i ka hua, iloko ona kona hua ma kona ano iho: a pela io no.

12 A hoouliu mai la ka honua i ka mauu, a me ka launahele e hua ana i ka hua ma kona ano iho, a me ka laau, e hua ana i ka hua, iloko ona kona hua ma kona ano iho: nana iho la ke Akua, ua maikai.

13 A o ke ahiahi a me ke kakahiaka, o ke kolu ia o ka la.

14 I iho la ke Akua, I mau malamalama iloko o ke aouli o ka lani, i mea hookaawale i ke ao a me ka po; i mau hoailona lakou no na kau, a no na la, a me na makahiki:

15 I mau kukui hoi lakou iloko o ke aouli o ka lani, e

1

# Chapter Seven

## Sexual Serial Killer and Cannibal

### Jeffrey Lionel Dahmer

On May 21, 1960 in Milwaukee, Wisconsin, Joyce and Lionel Dahmer became proud parents of their firstborn son, Jeffrey Lionel. His youngest years were that of an ordinary child with a father in university[119] and a working mother. When Jeffrey entered grade school, his mother's health began to decline, and she often became bedridden for prolonged periods. Joyce became addicted to tranquilizers and even tried suicide using this drug. Jeffrey felt that his parents argued continually throughout this period of his life.

At school, Jeffrey made a few friends despite his reserved and uncommunicative personality. At home, he became interested in dead insects, collecting and storing many in jars, including butterflies and dragonflies. This moved into collecting dead animals from the roadside which he then dismembered. He stored some body parts in jars in the family's toolshed and mounted some carcasses and skulls to trees and crosses in the woodland behind their house.

By 1968, they had moved twice, now living in Bath, Ohio. Lionel was pleased that his son showed interest in chemistry when he asked over a chicken dinner what would

---

[119] Working on a degree in chemistry

happen to chicken bones when placed in a bleach solution. So, he taught Jeffery proper use of a bleach solution to preserve the animal bones he still avidly collected.

Jeffrey's peers at Revere High School considered him an outcast with few friends. Most knew he drank beer and hard

alcohol, even smuggling it into school, calling it his "medicine." Teachers felt him intelligent though still largely uncommunicative. As a young teen he began having gay thoughts and fantasies including ideas of attacking and making a stranger unconscious to rape him. By his final high school years his grades had declined, possibly due to his increasing alcohol consumption. Home life also worsened as his parent's fighting led to separation and divorce in 1978.

Jeffrey graduated high school in May of 1978. His father had moved out of the family home earlier that year and then his mother moved away to Chippewa Falls, Wisconsin, taking his younger brother with her.[120] As a legal adult, no one questioned leaving Jeffrey on his own in the former family home.

Three weeks after his graduation, at age 18, Jeffrey committed his first murder by luring a hitchhiker named Steven Hicks to his home to drink beer and listen to music. Hours later he bludgeoned him to death with a dumbbell before masturbating over the corpse. Over a period of weeks, he meticulously dissolved the flesh in acid before flushing it and crushed the bones, scattering them in a nearby woodland.

---

[120] Jeffrey's younger brother was born on December 18, 1966 and his mother allowed Jeffrey to name him – he chose the name David.

Jeffrey had removed all trace of the murder before his father returned to the house with his new fiancée six weeks later.

Jeffrey enrolled in Ohio State University but dropped out months later to enroll in the US Army,[121] training as a medical specialist. There he raped two other soldiers, who were unwilling to report him. While superiors considered him "average to slightly above average," his performance began to decline over the course of that year – blamed on his alcohol abuse. Though judged unsuitable for military service, they gave him an honorable discharge about a year later[122] and a plane ticket to anywhere in the country. After a short stint in Miami Beach, he returned to his father's home in Ohio.

After a drunk and disorderly charge, Jeffrey's father sent him to live with his grandmother in West Allis, Wisconsin. She lovingly cared for him and he responded by doing chores, limited his drinking, and even accompanied her to church. He also sought work and gained employment as a phlebotomist at the Milwaukee Blood Plasma Center. However, it didn't last. About 10 months later police arrested Jeffrey for exposing himself to a crowd of 25 women and children.[123] He was laid off from his employment shortly after. It was two and half years before Jeffrey again found work, this time on a night shift at a chocolate factory.

---

[121] January 1979

[122] March 24, 1981

[123] His August 7, 1982, arrest resulted in a conviction and a $50 fine.

In 1985, Jeffrey's behavior started to spiral out of control. This included petty theft and regularly visiting Milwaukee's gay bars, bookstores, and bathhouses, and having sex with multiple partners. He viewed them as sex objects and found their movement during sex frustrating. By 1986, he would slip sleeping pills into their alcohol and rape their unconscious bodies. After a dozen complaints, the gay bathhouses revoked his membership. After reading about a coming funeral for an 18-year-old male, he decided to steal the freshly buried corpse to take home. Jeffrey only abandoned this plan when he found the soil too hard to dig up the coffin. Another indecent exposure charge soon followed.[124]

Jeffrey's urge to kill resurfaced in November of 1987. In a rented hotel room, he again pummeled a man to death – this time Steven Tuomi. Drawing on his earlier experience, he dismembered the body, storing the pieces at his grandmother's house and then dissolving or pulverizing the remains for disposal. For a time, he kept Toumi's severed head to perform sex acts with it, before also pulverizing and disposing of it too.

Jeffery's habit of bringing young men to the house, plus foul smells from the basement and garage, caused his grandmother to expel Jeffrey from her home in 1988. That same year, authorities charged him with drugging and fondling a 13-year-old boy, leading to second-degree assault conviction in January of 1989. He remained free before his scheduled sentencing in May. Two months before this sentencing Jeffrey murdered his fifth victim, Anthony Sears, disposing of the body in his usual manner. This time he preserved his victim's head and genitalia in acetone.

On May 23, 1989, the court sentenced Jeffrey to five-year probation and one year in the house of correction – but with work release so he could keep his job. For the first time, authorities forced him to register as a sex offender. His limited

---

[124] This charge was reduced to disorderly conduct and, on March 10, 1987, resulted in a year's probation with a recommendation he seek counseling.

imprisonment ended two months early. On release, he recovered his last victim's preserved and hidden remains.

May 14, 1990, marked the beginning of Jeffrey's continuing descent in sadistic sexually perverted murder. On that day, he strangled Raymond Smith with his bare hands; this time, spray-painting and saving Smith's skull. A few weeks later Edward Smooth died by Jeffrey's hands in a similar manner. Here, he tried a new method to preserve body parts, but accidentally exploded the skull in his oven. Three months later, he slashed the neck of Ernest Miller, enameled his head to preserve it, and ate portions of the body including his heart. Jeffrey's last murder of 1990 was David Thomas. He photographed his dismembering procedure but destroyed all the remains. For the next five months he often expressed suicidal thoughts.

February of 1991 saw Jeffrey resume his murders. As he later testified, the compulsion to kill "just filled my thoughts all day long." There's mostly no need to provide further details as he continued to rape, strangle, dismember and commit sex acts with the remains. He continued to keep body parts as trophies. Over a six-month period, Jeffrey murdered Curtis Straughter, Errol Lindsey, Tony Hughes, Konerak Sinthasomphone, Matt Turner, Oliver Lacy, and Joseph Bradehoft. In Konerak's case, Jeffrey drilled a hole in his skull and injected hydrochloric acid into his brain. Still alive the next day, he managed to escape. Three women found him outside of Jeffrey's apartment bleeding from his buttocks. The now arrived Jeffrey convinced the responding police that they were lovers and Konerak's condition was temporary disorientation. The officers helped Jeffrey lead Konerak back into the apartment, rebuking the women's protests telling them not to interfere with this domestic incident. Konerak was dead from more hydrochloric acid the next day.

Jeffrey's next intended victim, Tracy Edwards, managed to escape on July 22, 1991, finally leading to Jeffrey's arrest in his apartment. The arresting officers found his collection of severed body parts. As one of the arresting officers, Robert Rauth, pinned Jeffrey to the ground to prevent his attempted escape, he heard him mutter "For what I did I should be dead." The chief medical examiner stated the scene was "more like dismantling someone's museum than an actual crime scene." The next day, Jeffrey waived his right to a lawyer and confessed to killing all 17 young men.

In January of 1992, Jeffrey pled guilty but insane to all these counts of murder. After intensive medical and psychiatric examination, on February 15, 1993, the court ruled that he was

completely sane during his crimes. His guilty verdicts sent him to prison for life plus seventy years. Jeffrey spent the first year of his imprisonment in solitary confinement over concerns about his physical safety by fellow inmates.

Shortly after Jeffrey's arrest and confession, a police detective gave him a copy of the Bible. About three years later, after Jeffrey was in the regular prison population, he appeared in a television interview where he expressed his wish that he could "find a little peace."[125] One Oklahoman believer watching, Curt Booth, thought "I know somebody who can give you that peace. His name is Jesus Christ." Booth himself had served four years in a Kansas prison. He studied the Bible while behind bars but didn't come to faith until he hit bottom as a drug and alcohol abuser following his release from prison. Booth knew that Jesus could save the worst.

Booth sent Jeffrey materials teaching him more about the Bible and about God's salvation. Jeffrey wrote back thanking him. Further, he told Booth that he had believed and

---

[125] April 1994

now wanted baptism. Jeffrey also started to read other Christian materials included from the Institute for Creation Research.

Booth worked to find a pastor with access to the prison who would meet with Jeffrey and baptize him. Most contacted pastors were "scared to go in." But one pastor, Roy Ratcliff, from Wisconsin, set up weekly meetings with Jeffrey. Ratcliff remembers Jeffrey saying he feared the pastor's first visit. "He dreaded that I might say, 'No, you're too evil. You're too sinful.'"[126] Now persuaded that Jeffrey had put his faith in Jesus, Ratcliff baptized him on May 10, 1994.

Another believer who heard about Jeffrey's newfound faith wrote to congratulate him. Jeffrey replied to David Hartman and sent him $5 worth of stamps, asking him to mail him 25 copies of the Bible course he had originally received. He wanted to share this with other inmates! In the same letter Jeffrey mentioned an attack in prison.[127] "I don't know if you heard, but last Sunday I was attacked while in the chapel," he wrote. "Some guy[128] tried to cut my throat open with a razor but didn't succeed. The razor broke, and my neck was only slightly scratched. I believe that it was only the protective grace of our Great Lord & Savior Jesus Christ that saved me from serious injury or death!"

That brush with death aside, Jeffrey no longer feared what might happen to him. For months, his daily assigned work detail was cleaning the prison toilet block. On the morning of November 28, 1994, Jeffrey began his work detail with two fellow inmates, Jesse Anderson and Christopher Scarver. In the bathroom, Scarver beat Jeffrey and Jesse to death with a 20-inch metal bar.

---

[126] Roy wrote a book about his experience with Jeffrey, *Dark Journey, Deep Grace: Jeffrey Dahmer's Story of Faith.*

[127] July 1994

[128] That guy was prisoner Osvaldo Durruthy.

Jeffrey Lionel Dahmer is perhaps the worst mass murderer you've heard of. Few believers could meet with this sex offender and serial killer once he became a repentant believer in Jesus Christ. Some mocked the idea that such a horrible person could find peace with God, casually calling this a "jailhouse conversion" as if to cheapen or nullify his decision by its location. Other people said, "if this man's going to be in heaven I don't want to be there." I'm glad some believers were willing to share the good news of Christ with him, and that others took time to correspond with Jeffrey and encourage him in his new faith. I'm also grateful Pastor Roy Ratcliff was willing to set aside his fear and spent time with Jeffrey in person. What about you? If given the opportunity would you have visited this man?

**Matthew 25:31** "When the Son of Man comes in his glory, and all the angels with him, then he will sit on his glorious throne. 32 Before him will be gathered all the nations, and he will separate people one from another as a shepherd separates the sheep from the goats. 33 And he will place the sheep on his right, but the goats on the left. 34 Then the King will say to those on his right, 'Come, you who are blessed by my Father, inherit the kingdom prepared for you from the foundation of the world. 35 For I was hungry and you gave me food, I was thirsty and you gave me drink, I was a stranger and you welcomed me, 36 I was naked and you clothed me, I was sick and you visited me, I was in prison and you came to me.' 37 Then the righteous will answer him, saying, 'Lord, when did we see you hungry and feed you, or thirsty and give you drink? 38 And when did we see you a stranger and welcome you, or naked and clothe you? 39 And when did we see you sick or in prison and visit you?' 40 And the King will answer them, 'Truly, I say to you, as you did it to one of the least of these my brothers, you did it to me.' 41 "Then he will say to those on his left, 'Depart from me, you cursed, into the eternal fire prepared for the devil and his angels. 42 For I was hungry and you gave me no food, I was thirsty and you gave me no drink, 43 I was a stranger and you did not welcome me, naked and you did not clothe me, sick and in prison and you did not visit me.' 44 Then they also will answer, saying, 'Lord, when did we see you hungry or thirsty or a stranger or naked or sick or in prison, and did not minister to you?' [45] Then he will answer them, saying, 'Truly, I say to you, as you did not do it to one of the least of these, you did not do it to me.' [46] And these will go away into eternal punishment, but the righteous into eternal life."

# Chapter Eight

## Domestic Terrorists and Religious Jihadis

In early first century Israel, most Jews hated the burdensome occupation of their land by the Romans and their puppet client kings, namely the Herod family.[129] While some enriched themselves and sought power or wealth through their collaboration with these occupying powers, far more prayed for freedom and quietly tolerated their predicament. Others made the choice to actively seek their freedom, whatever the cost. An early hero of their movement – some say their founder – was Judas of Galilee, who fought against an early Roman taxation census.[130] He understood that God meant Jews to be free with only Him as the Ruler and Lord. Judas had encouraged people to slight the Romans and not register – and to make sure they didn't register, everyone that did became fair game as Roman collaborators. Judas and his followers would then burn collaborators' houses and confiscate their livestock.

---

[129] Rome installed Herod, son of Antipater the Idumean, as King of the Jews in 37 AD and affirmed three of his immediate surviving descendants as lesser regional rulers following his death.

[130] Acts 5:37 ... Judas the Galilean rose up in the days of the census and drew away some of the people after him.

## Simon the Zealot

Simon[131] joined this Jewish freedom movement as a young man. Though now decades after Judas of Galilee's brutal martyrdom for their cause by Roman hands, his movement, now called the Zealots[132], continued to be a subversive thorn in the Roman's side. Simon was sure Israel could finally gain their freedom if only enough Jews would join their cause. Israel needed to stand up together to overthrow their Roman yoke. Simon, like all Zealots, was passionate for the Law and mostly sympathetic to the Pharisee's strict teachings. He believed God would again bless Israel if people would only better follow the Law as taught by the Pharisees. They especially hated idolatry and those pagan Romans had idols everywhere. All Herodian rulers were soft on idolatry. He had heard these kings even made offerings in the idol-filled temples of pagan Roman gods while visiting cities outside Israel.

Simon would've considered joining the Pharisees, but they were all talk, and he agreed with the Zealots that much more action was necessary. Besides, most Pharisees scorned the Zealots. Pharisees called Zealots *Biryonim*, or wild ruffians, because they wouldn't follow the Jewish leaders. Simon felt

---

[131] Simon the Zealot, not to be confused with Simon Peter, is mentioned in Scriptures in Matthew 10:4, Mark 3:18, Luke 6:15, and Acts 1:13.

[132] First century historian Josephus in his *Antiquities of the Jews* records there were primarily three main Jewish sects, the Pharisees, the Sadducees, and the Essenes. The Zealots became a fourth sect, founded by Judas of Galilee (also called Judas of Gamala) as he fought Roman tax reform shortly after the Roman government converted Herod Archelaus' territory into a Roman province directly under their rule in 6 AD. Josephus noted that the Zealots "agree in all other things with the Pharisaic notions; but they have an inviolable attachment to liberty, and say that God is to be their only Ruler and Lord. (Antiquities 18.1.6)"

that those leaders, including the Sanhedrin, were nothing but corrupt sons of darkness.[133]

Some Zealots were willing to kill for their cause, though inflicting pain was their normal style. Most settled for harassing Romans or Jewish collaborators – often by "confiscating" their belongings or sabotaging their livelihoods. Those that chose to kill collaborators became a related group known as the Sicarii, or daggermen. Their name came from their weapon of choice. This group of Zealot assassins would mingle with crowds during festivals, slip up behind  their selected victim, and then draw their Sicarii – a short curved knife – from under their cloak and quickly execute their target. Not only did it remove collaborators, the terror it provoked effectively disrupted the Roman government.

While Simon wasn't personally willing to go as far as the Sicarii, he sympathized with their goals. And, for those claiming the Sicarii violated the Mosaic Law by committing murder, most Zealots justified their actions because "this was war." The goal justified the means – even as it did with the Zealot's theft of goods from these misguided and vile Roman collaborators. Simon knew and accepted the possible cost of being a rebel. If caught, Zealot or Sicarii, the guaranteed results included Roman torture and a probable gruesome death.

Simon became Jesus' disciple because Jesus selected

---

[133] The separatist Essenes at Qumran had long declared the Jewish leadership in Jerusalem as "sons of darkness." While this monastic group spent their time hiding in the desert, most knew they called for a coming war between the sons of light and the sons of darkness.

him. He had always wondered why. In his time with Jesus, he came to see how God fulfilled His Law in Jesus Christ. In the events surrounding Jesus' betrayal he learned an important lesson. God didn't want His people to fight using earthly swords.[134] Oh, and on the day of Jesus' crucifixion, he knew of the man released that day. Authorities had arrested Barabbas, whose real name only a few knew, for robbery and murder.[135] And Pilate had released this criminal instead of Jesus. Simon's hope was that this Zealot Sicarii could find true freedom through believing in Jesus Christ. He realized if it wasn't for Jesus showing him the true way,[136] this could have been him.

Simon, no longer a Zealot terrorist, now a passionate believer and Apostle of Jesus Christ, lived the rest of his days spreading God's good news. Many early church gatherings welcomed him during his travels. Though records are uncertain, verbal accounts record his death as a martyr for the testimony of Jesus.

## Saul of Tarsus

Saul's birth took place about a year before the first

---

[134] See Luke 22:36 and Matthew 26:51-53. John confirms one of the two bearing swords was Simon Peter (John 18:10). It's probable that Simon the Zealot was the other armed disciple. As a former Zealot he would have likely carried a short sword, such as the Sicarii, even if he wasn't willing to use it as they did.

[135] Barabbas means "Son of a Father," an ancient equivalent to John Doe. This "notorious" individual is mentioned in Matthew 27:16-26. Mark identifies the greater charges against him as "murder" and "insurrection" (Mark 15:7). John confirms the other usual charge against a Zealot, that of robbery (John 18:40).

[136] See John 14:6.

Zealot rebelled against Rome. [137] His birthplace was Tarsus, the capital city of the Roman province of Cilicia in a first century Asia Minor.[138] Saul's father had named him after Israel's first king, perhaps the most prominent patriarch in their tribe of Benjamin – Benjamin being a great-grandson of Abraham himself.

While an ancient and prosperous trading center, most knew Saul's hometown as the site of Cleopatra's first seductive meeting with Marc Antony half a century earlier.[139] Others were quick to point out Tarsus' great centers of learning, with its featured academy that produced the philosopher tutor of the first Roman Emperor, Caesar Augustus. This latter tie guaranteed continuous imperial patronage[140] for the city.

---

[137] Many scholars estimate Paul's birth was in 5 AD, a few say as much as 10 years earlier, but this makes it a stretch for him to be referred to as a "young man" at Stephen's stoning. See Acts 7:58.

[138] See Acts 22:3. Tarsus is located on the southern coast of modern Turkey.

[139] Cleopatra VII Philopator was the last active ruler of the Ptolemaic Kingdom of Egypt. Marcus Antonius, or Mark Antony, was a Roman politician (Triumvir and Proconsul) and general. Antony and Octavian (later Caesar Augustus) came to civil war, with the latter winning. Antony and Cleopatra fled to Egypt, where they committed suicide.

[140] Patronage was a hierarchical relationship rooted in ancient Roman society and customs. Patronage ("clientela") was a two-way relationship between greater and lesser parties, the patron ("patronus") and their client ("cliens"). While originally between individuals, by the time of the empire this expanded to include groups and entire cities as clients. The wealthy patron used their rank, wealth, power, or prestige, to provide protection ("patrocinium") and

Saul's family was distinctly Jewish, his father a Pharisee.[141] But his father was also a Roman citizen, something relatively rare for an early first century Jew. This coveted status granted him easy and free access across provincial borders and aided in business. His father's membership in the Pharisaical sect guaranteed Saul a strict upbringing, with his father wanting him to also be zealous for God's law. Admittedly, it was difficult to keep such zeal while living among the vast Gentile majority in this Roman province. His father always lamented that Saul's first language was Greek, so he had worked hard to

---

benefits to their client. In return, the client was honor and duty bound to support the patron.

On a personal level, a client's benefits might include loans, influence in business deals and even marriage, representation in court, or support for priesthood or political office. The client was expected to offer their services to their patron as needed and demanded. A client and patron couldn't sue each other or bear witness against each other in court. If a client died without an heir, the patron could inherit their property. If a patron was taken prisoner, their client was obligated to pay ransom. Some became clients of multiple patrons, causing potential problems when interests conflicted between patrons.

Augustus' genius as emperor was making himself a patron of all Romans. Beyond this broad relationship, he entered into a patron-client relationship with groups of soldiers, trade unions, and cities alike throughout the empire. These groups became duty-bound to support the emperor at all costs, while he bestowed special favors, funds, and honors on these clients. A city receiving imperial patronage had protection and some relief from the tax collector. This patronage could include receipt of Roman citizenship, a valuable status. Augustus' immense personal wealth provided him ample means for a multitude of patronages. Augustus' successors sought to assume and continue these patronages.

[141] "A son of Pharisees." See Acts 23:6.

make sure that Saul also learned Hebrew from an early age.

Being a Pharisee and Jewish law teacher wasn't a paying career in or out of Israel, so Saul's father – along with other Pharisees– held other work. Saul, from an early age, also trained in his father's occupation, namely tent making. Their home province of Cilicia was famous for producing and exporting goat-hair cloth, something highly sought after for quality tent making. In fact, the long hair used for this cloth only came from goats native to this area. In this world of trade, Saul had little use for Hebrew as Greek was the everyday business language. But this was only commerce; Saul's soul concerned his father more than his income.

Saul's father sent both his sister and him to Jerusalem.[142] Here Saul could continue his Pharisaical studies under the best teacher available. Finally, Saul would get to use the Hebrew he had learned. His sister would now live in a place with more respect for godly women. Her father's goal, of course, included her marriage to a good Jew from Jerusalem, with hopes of him being a Pharisee.

Saul's teacher was Gamaliel, grandson of the renowned teacher Hillel. When it came to learning Torah, there were only two schools of thought, Shammai or Hillel, and Saul's father thought Hillel superior. Gamaliel was now Nasi and Rabban, meaning Prince and Our Master of Jerusalem's Great Sanhedrin, the Jew's ruling body. [143] This meant Saul was

---

[142] In Acts 23:16 Paul's young nephew and married sister are shown to live in Jerusalem.

[143] The Jewish Mishnah portrays Gamaliel as one of the Israel's greatest teachers: "Once Rabban Gamaliel the Elder died, the glory of Torah ceased, while purity and abstinence disappeared. (Sotah

learning from the best.[144]

Saul was a young man in Jerusalem during Jesus of Nazareth's crucifixion. Of course, he had heard of this troublesome man and his contempt for the religious leaders, including his instructor Gamaliel. Gamaliel thought it unwise for any of his pupils to see or hear Jesus, reluctantly admitting that even their best teachers of the Law had trouble in their conversations with Jesus.[145]

Even without hearing Jesus for himself, Saul felt He got what He deserved for inciting the people against these godly rulers. And he couldn't believe that Jesus' disciples had tried to perpetuate the fraud that He had risen from the grave. No one survived these brutal public Roman executions, as the empire was unrivaled in their perfected execution technique. Saul knew with certainty Jesus' disciples had merely spirited away his body to set up this resurrection myth. Witnesses testified to this inventive hoax.[146]

---

9:15)"

[144] Acts 22:3 "I am a Jew, born in Tarsus in Cilicia, but brought up in this city, educated at the feet of Gamaliel according to the strict manner of the law of our fathers, being zealous for God as all of you are this day.

[145] See Luke 20:19-40 "... they no longer dared to ask him any question."

[146] Matthew 28:11 ... behold, some of the guard went into the city and told the chief priests all that had taken place. [12] And when they had assembled with the elders and taken counsel, they gave a sufficient sum of money to the soldiers [13] and said, "Tell people, 'His disciples came by night and stole him away while we were asleep.' [14] And if this comes to the governor's ears, we will satisfy him and keep you out of trouble." [15] So they took the money and did as they were directed. And this story has been spread among the Jews to this day.

Over the next few months, all Saul heard about were these followers of "The Way," people persistently claiming Jesus was alive. He felt the division they were causing was a threat to Judaism itself. Though his teacher Gamaliel was publicly more tolerant of these schismatics[147] Saul heard their often-heated discussions over possible and permanent solutions to this increasing problem. He sided with those wanting more action.

Saul was present when members dragged a vocal member of "The Way," a man named Stephen, before the Sanhedrin. Reports said Stephen was a deacon in this new movement.[148] Charges against Stephen were serious: multiple witnesses from the Synagogue of the Freedmen testified that he had blasphemed Moses and God. In the questioning, Stephen had put on a good show reciting his knowledge of Jewish history. But did he really think he was better than the esteemed teachers of this council? Did he think he could teach the esteemed Gamaliel anything? In the end, his long defense didn't matter. This blasphemer had betrayed himself by claiming the heretic Jesus equal to God. The Council and those present were so enraged they carried Stephen outside the city and stoned him to death, as he deserved.[149] Saul's momentary concern was what the Roman's would say about this spontaneous execution. He well knew Roman law bound the Council to get permission for any execution as only the Roman governor had the right to give such an order.

In the eyes of the council, Saul was a young man, only in his late twenties. Tradition demanded all members of this great council be of "advanced age." While Saul had joined the crowd for Stephen's execution, he felt it wasn't his place to

---

[147] Gamaliel's restraint appears in a later event recorded in Scriptures: see Acts 5:33-40. It stopped them from killing the apostles but allowed the apostles to be beaten.

[148] See Acts 6:1-6.

[149] Stephen's full story is in Acts 6:8-7:60.

fully take part. So, he did what he could by taking care of his elders' outer garments. Saul worried that some might think his reserved participation meant he didn't agree with what they did. In the days which followed, he made clear that he wholeheartedly agreed with this necessary execution.

In the following weeks, Saul became convinced he needed to do more to stop this pestilent sect called "The Way." He heard that some of its Jerusalem members had fled to Damascus. Who knew what trouble they could stir up against the Jewish leaders in the city housing the Roman Imperial Legate?[150] The

---

[150] A Roman Imperial Legate ("legatus") was a high-ranking military officer in the Roman army, in modern terms a military general. Under Augustus, the legate was an officer in command of a legion. The legate received a large share of any military rewards or spoils from successful campaigns, making this office a lucrative one. High ranking political figures, including Roman consuls, often desired and attained these positions. From Augustus onward there were levels within these legates. The lowest level was the former military tribune, now called the "legatus legionis," the senior commander of the army over the centurions. In the east, including Mesopotamia and Egypt, of similar authority with the "legatus legionis," legions were commanded by "praefectus legionis," these were normally of the equestrian rank. The supreme commander of both of these lower level legates was the "legatus augusti pro praetore." If the region only had a single legion, this "legatus augusti" held direct command of the legion while serving as the provincial governor. These officers were former well-connected politicians, specifically tribunes, each normally appointed directly by the emperor. Their term was originally limited to a two-year period, but emperors later expanded this to three or four years and occasionally more. Syria was one of about a dozen provinces ruled by a "legatus augusti." Capital punishment was the prerogative of all legates under Roman law. Legates were readily recognizable in appearance by their elaborate helmet, body armor, waist band ("cincticulus"), and his scarlet cloak fastened onto one shoulder ("paludamentum").

governor of Syria was the highest regional authority and even Pontius Pilate, prefect of Judea,[151] had to defer to him. Saul's anger against The Way grew daily. He heard enough to know the Sadducean High Priest, Joseph ben Caiaphas, was also of the same mind. Caiaphas feared Christian protests to the Syrian governor, over some supposedly unjust execution, could make it to Rome and risk his position. Caiaphas' term as High Priest was no longer for life as the Mosaic Law demanded. This made his cooperation with Rome the only guarantee for an extended

---

[151] A Roman prefect was a regional governor serving under the authority of that province's Roman Imperial Legate. Pilate, as prefect of Judea ("praefectus Iudaeae"), was subordinate to the military "legatus augusti" over the Roman province of Syria. While political in nature, the prefect's office was of relatively low prestige. His troops were more for policing than military actions. The prefect headed the local judicial system, directly hearing cases and appeals, and could inflict capital punishment unless overruled by the legate. Collecting taxes, minting coins, and distributing government funds were part of his administrative functions. The office of Syrian legate was empty for the first six years of Pilate's rule, so he mostly governed as he pleased. Pilate collided with the power of the Syrian legate in these later final years of his tenure, finally being removed from office and sent to Rome for trial before the emperor. Since Rome allowed limited local control to the Jews, Pilate officially shared a narrow amount of civil and religious power with the Jewish Sanhedrin. To control the Jewish high priest, Rome gave the prefect the right to appoint or depose the high priest. Also, the prefect controlled the high priest's robes, only allowing him to wear them for official religious functions. Showing Caiaphas was Pilate's reliable ally, he kept Caiaphas in office during his entire tenure. Confirming Rome's knowledge of this alliance, Caiaphas was quickly deposed following Pilate's forced removal from office.

term and stability for the Jewish people.[152]

Neglecting his teacher Gamaliel's restraint, Saul went straight to the High Priest and convinced him to grant him permission to track down these cowardly blasphemers in Damascus, whether men or women. Officials quickly drafted for Saul to show he was acting under official authority. Returning these problems to Jerusalem would guarantee their imprisonment and, as necessary, permanent silencing. [153]

Though Saul called himself a zealot for God[154], he never thought himself anything like those contemptible religious terrorists known as Zealots. Unlike those misguided fools, his zeal for God was genuine and approved by the authorities. He assured himself he was no lawbreaker like them.

Saul never expected what happened on the road to Damascus. In blazing light, Jesus showed himself to Saul and spoke with him.[155] Those traveling with Saul heard Jesus' voice but couldn't see who spoke. When Jesus finished speaking, Saul now saw nothing – nothing at all – as the light had blinded him. But he could never forget what he had last seen. Saul knew without a doubt that Jesus was alive. He felt great shame for how he had formerly treated Jesus' followers. He

---

[152] Rome or her designated rulers, whether of the Herodian family or a Roman prefect, now appointed or deposed High Priests at will.

[153] Acts 22:4 I persecuted this Way to the death, binding and delivering to prison both men and women, 5 as the high priest and the whole council of elders can bear me witness. From them I received letters to the brothers, and I journeyed toward Damascus to take those also who were there and bring them in bonds to Jerusalem to be punished.

[154] Greek "Zelotes." See Acts 22:3 and Galatians 1:14.

[155] Paul's full conversion experience is found in Acts 9:1-16.

could hardly believe that Jesus later sent one of them in Damascus, a man named Ananias, to heal his blindness. How could this man call him "brother" after all he had done to persecute the church?[156] And yet, Ananias went on to confirm Jesus' appointment of Saul to spread His good news to Jews, Gentiles, and rulers alike.

**1 Corinthians 15:8** Last of all, as to one untimely born, he appeared also to me. [9] For I am the least of the apostles, unworthy to be called an apostle, because I persecuted the church of God. [10] But by the grace of God I am what I am, and his grace toward me was not in vain.

Saul was a changed and changing man – now struggling to do right by the indwelling power of God.[157] Over the next few years God taught him what to say and how to say it with boldness. While Saul longed to spend more time among his people, the Jews, he rarely visited Jerusalem. Most of the time, Saul lived among Gentiles and visited Jewish diaspora scattered throughout the greater Roman world. These new friends mostly knew him only by the Latin transliteration of his Hebrew name, Paul.[158] Over the following decades Paul learned what God meant in the message He had given Ananias, that He would show Paul how much he would suffer for the

---

[156] See Acts 9:17

[157] See Romans 7:21-25.

[158] We know Saul is interchangeably called Paul for the first time on the island of Cyprus, quite some time after his conversion, see Acts 13:9. Showing most subsequently knew him only by the name Paul, he then refers to himself only by this name when he later writes all his letters. Regardless, some in the church and outside of it, and even the Holy Spirit, call him Saul long after his conversion (see Acts 9:17, 11:25, 11:30, 12:25, 13:2, 13:7).

sake of Jesus' name.[159]

Amid beatings, shipwrecks, and imprisonment, Paul never looked back.[160] He lived the rest of his life trusting in Jesus, assured of Jesus' love and continuous presence.

**Romans 8:37** No, in all these things we are more than conquerors through him who loved us. [38] For I am sure that neither death nor life, nor angels nor rulers, nor things present nor things to come, nor powers, [39] nor height nor depth, nor anything else in all creation, will be able to separate us from the love of God in Christ Jesus our Lord.

Paul finally died for his testimony to the grace of Jesus Christ, beheaded by order of the emperor Nero. Shortly before his death he wrote:

**2 Timothy 4:6** For I am already being poured out as a drink offering, and the time of my departure has come. [7] I have fought the good fight, I have finished the race, I have kept the

---

[159] See Acts 9:16

[160] See 2 Corinthians 11:24-28

faith.

    In later years, believers sometimes feared being around Paul, but never because of his past. Rather they feared the authorities would treat them the same as Paul.[161] Apart from those times, Paul spent many occasions enjoying fellowship with Gentile and Jewish believers, some for extended periods.

    Are you willing to identify with this man, a vile sinner[162], once willing to imprison and kill Christians in the

---

[161] 2 Timothy 4:16 "... no one came to stand by me, but all deserted me."

[162] 1 Timothy 1:15 The saying is trustworthy and deserving of full acceptance, that Christ Jesus came into the world to save sinners, of whom I am the foremost. [16] But I received mercy for this reason, that in me, as the foremost, Jesus Christ might display his perfect patience as an example to those who were to believe in him for eternal life. [17] To the King of the ages, immortal, invisible, the only God, be honor

name of religion? Are you willing to read his books?

God used him to write the largest portion of the Bible in the shortest period of any other author.[163]

---

and glory forever and ever. Amen.

[163] Paul wrote over half of the New Testament during a 17-year period. About half of this was written over a 3-year period including Philemon, Colossians, Ephesians, Philippians, Hebrews, 1 Timothy, and Titus. He composed four of these letters while in prison.

# Chapter Nine

## The Devil's Baby

### Byang Henry Kato

Only two of Heri and Zawi Kato's children lived. Following their first born, Byang Henry, eight additional children died except one. Home for Byang was Kwoi, a Jaba village of about 15,000 people, in Kaduna State of Nigeria. Pagan worshippers in the village saw his unlikely survival as proof of their fetish worship, that "the Devil (*Kuno*) was looking after his baby."[164] Kato's parents followed Juju, a religion scattered throughout Nigeria and Ghana. Juju demands blood sacrifices, even human sacrifices. Torture and fear are key elements controlling its participants, subjugating women and children. Its practitioners are often described as "hardhearted, cruel, wicked, and bloodthirsty."[165] Not only did his father name him "Byang," meaning "You hate me," a few months after his birth on June 23, 1936, Heri dedicated Byang

---

[164] *The Devil's Baby*, Africa Now, January-March 1962

[165] *A Portrait of Dr. Byang H. Kato*, Africa Journal of Evangelical Theology, Volume 15.2 1996, By Christien M. Breman

to become a Juju priest. This wasn't unexpected. Heri belonged to the *Pop-ku* family (the fetish priest family) of Sabzuro.[166] He proudly dedicated Byang to serve the Devil while he was still a baby. The entire Jaba tribe expected him to become a Juju priest.

Despite constant sickness and malnutrition, Kato survived. His father regularly trained him in the ways of Juju and its fetish practices. He taught him to make grain offerings to the spirits of the sacred sycamore trees and the art of blood sacrifices. Byang's early ambition was also to become the expected Juju priest. At ten years old, Byang went through tribal initiations tied to Juju. Surviving this required indifference to physical suffering and spiritual progress in seeing "Juju." This initiation was considered necessary for him to become a "real man." Together with 300 other boys, they were sent into the jungle for a week. Living in caves by day and roaming the forest by night, they were to survive and learn the ways of Juju. Village elders told the women that Juju had swallowed the boys and the women must bring food and wine so that Juju could eat until its stomach was full. Only then would Juju vomit out their sons.

In the jungle, the boys were forced to eat food mixed with filth. Indoctrination continued day and night combined with oath-taking. Those who could see Juju best, having a good imagination such as Byang, received only a few cane beatings. Those who couldn't were beaten mercilessly. After seven days, the boys were marched home to a great feast and celebration including many animal and bird sacrifices. These boys had learned the spiritual secret of *dodo* and had been warned, on pain of death, that such secrets could never be revealed to women. The joyous celebration and singing were mingled with the wailing of some parents realizing their sons failed to survive this initiation and had been "kept by the Juju." Juju had its human sacrifices. And Byang Henry Kato was well on his way to becoming a Juju priest.

---

[166] *Byang Kato: Ambassador for Christ*, Biography of Dr Byang H. Kato by Sophie de la Haye, 1986

Shortly after his Juju initiation Byang saw missionary Mary Haas, from the Sudan Interior Mission, when she came to his part of town many times each month. She taught about Jesus in the Jaba language and she had a "black box." This "black box" was a record player that could sing and talk Hausa, another common language of the area often used in trade. Byang wanted to see the people talking and singing inside the box. A Christian boy then asked him to come with him to the Sudan Interior Mission School in Kwoi. Intrigued, at age eleven, Byang went. It was so different, with meetings filled with singing and recitations of Bible verses, that he returned day after day. Byang's parents were indifferent to this until he asked to not work on the farm on Sunday. For this request he was scolded and cursed – and they forced him to stop attending the school, saying his actions brought shame on the family by not worshipping Juju. Two years of persistence from the school's Pastor and other missionaries slowly won over Byang's parents and they finally allowed him to return to the school. Even Byang's grandfather announced: "Let him go. Times have changed."[167]

*Class 6 of the SIM Senior Primary School, Kwoi, 1954. Byang is in the back row, second from the right.*

---

[167] *Byang Kato: Ambassador for Christ*, Biography of Dr Byang H. Kato by Sophie de la Haye, 1986

It was at the Sudan Interior Mission School that Byang heard the gospel and responded to a teacher's invitation to trust in Jesus Christ as his Lord and Savior. He didn't realize all this meant. Byang's father was furious when he heard about his public commitment to Jesus Christ. He beat his son and refused him food and took his shirt away. Finally, he gave up on seeing his son become a Juju priest, when he saw Byang wouldn't reject Jesus. Though Byang could return to school, his father wouldn't support him. So, Byang worked a job to pay his own annual school fees,[168] buy necessary school clothes, school supplies, and books. In the morning he worked the fields for his father, in the afternoon he went to school and then to his part time job. At night, he started reading and studying, something hardly known in Africa. It paid off, and Byang was first in his classes during the last three years of Primary School. Having gained understanding of his Christian faith, Byang was baptized publicly, in a small stream, on November 21, 1948.

Byang knew he was a Christian but felt the next few years were full of constant failure. Youthful lusts and other influences tugged on him. He felt his testimony was "a mockery to the Name of Christ." It was during Pastor Gin's preaching in March of 1953 that Byang's heart was completely broken, now yielding his entire life to the Lord – publicly confessing his sins and committing to serve the Lord all the days of his life. At 17 years of age, Byang was willing to go and do whatever the Lord wanted. Over the next two years he overcame his fears, doubts, financial inadequacies, and much negative peer pressure, to attend Bible School and later enter full time ministry after graduation in 1957. He saw God provide through his hard work and through the miraculous generosity of other believers.

Byang didn't stop there. He became the first evangelical African Christian to earn a doctoral degree in theology. He uncompromisingly believed the African church should not compromise theological principles while at the

---

[168] School fees were $1.50 per year.

same time remaining distinctly African. He challenged the rise of universalism and syncretism within African theology and its churches.[169] He became known as the  Father of African Evangelicalism.[170] This "happy child of God" was "no longer the Devil's baby."[171] And, in contrast to his parents, Byang married a Christian woman and fathered three children.[172] These he dedicated to the Lord, promising God that he would provide for them spiritually and materially.[173] All three became believers in Jesus Christ.

Would you join with the multitude of African believers who welcomed this former devil worshipper into their church and homes?

---

[169] *The Legacy of Byang Kato*, internationalbulletin.org, 04/2004, by Keith Ferdinando

[170] His landmark work is: *Theological Pitfalls in Africa*, By Byang H. Kato B.D., Th. D., 1975. Its forward is by Dr. Billy Graham and its introduction is by Charles C. Ryrie.

[171] *The Devil's Baby*, Africa Now, January-March 1962

[172] Byang married Jummai Gandu, who had been raised by a godly believing grandmother. They married on January 26, 1957, a year before Byang completed Bible School.

[173] *A Portrait of Dr. Byang H. Kato*, Africa Journal of Evangelical Theology, Volume 15.2 1996, By Christien M. Breman

# Chapter Ten

## Hijacker and Thief

### Raffaele Minichiello

Raffaele Minichiello's earliest years were in the small village of Melito Irpino, slightly north and inland of coastal Naples, Italy. Though earthquake prone, this hilly area provided a great home until the early evening of August 21, 1962. A then unprecedented 6.1 magnitude earthquake rocked the area, with two powerful aftershocks. Together these left their village ruined and uninhabitable – and the family lost everything. No one, no authority, came to help and the family was on its own. Circumstances and uncertainty turned twelve-year-old Raffaele's life upside down.[174]

Raffaele's parents decided to leave Italy and immigrate to the United States to start over. Home became Seattle, Washington. Raffaele struggled with all this change and classmates often teased him for his thick accent and problems with speaking English. By 1967, he dropped out of high school and at age 17 traveled to San Diego for voluntary enlistment in

---

[174] To read more about Raffaele, see *A hijacked plane stopped in Bangor on its way to Rome 50 years ago this week*, The Bangor Daily News, 2019/10/30 and *TWA85: 'The world's longest and most spectacular hijacking'* by Roland Hughes, BBC News, 26 October 2019

the US Marine Corp. This ended his ambition of becoming a commercial pilot but provided him hope of becoming a naturalized American citizen. He soon found himself in

Vietnam during the worst of the war. He was a "grunt," someone dropped in the front line for a few months at a time. His only job was to kill and survive 120-degree (49 C) weather during monsoon season. While deployed, Raffaele sent money to a Marines saving fund, collecting and saving $800 (worth about $5,600 in 2020). He served proudly and well, with the government of South Vietnam awarding him the Cross of Gallantry. After being wounded, the army returned him to Camp Pendleton in California.

By then, Raffaele's father was suffering from terminal cancer and had returned to Italy to die, with his mother still in the US. He decided to use his savings to fly to Italy and visit his father one last time. Checking his account balance, he found only $600 – not enough for international travel. Raffaele sought help from his superiors, insisting they owed him the missing $200. These authorities dismissed his complaint. Blaming the military for shorting him this $200 (worth about $1,400 in 2020), he decided to correct this himself. So, one night in May of 1969, he got drunk and broke into Pendleton's post exchange to steal $200 worth of items. It was easy to justify – they owed it to him.

Eight beers later, Minichiello fell asleep inside the store, leading to authorities promptly arresting him the following morning. Facing burglary charges, he decided to go AWOL before his scheduled court martial and likely imprisonment. He still wanted to find a way to visit his father. But now, without enough funds, and as a wanted man, he headed to Los Angeles taking with him a Chinese rifle he had brought back as a war trophy from Vietnam.

The day after his scheduled Camp Pendleton court-martial, Raffaele booked himself on the October 30th TWA flight from Los Angeles to San Francisco (actually leaving at 1:30 am on Friday October 31). His ticket cost $15.50 (worth about $110 in 2020). Getting on the plane, Raffaele's clothing was military camouflage. He carried his M1 Rifle disassembled in his bag plus 250 rounds of ammunition. This was before the days of x-rays and metal detectors or even bag inspections. Still, one of the flight crew noticed a thin container protruding from the backpack of this nervous but polite young man. The crew readily accepted his answer that this was a fishing rod.

The mostly empty plane, with only 40 passengers on board, didn't notice Raffaele head to the restroom to assemble his rifle. Most were dozing in the early morning hours. Now only 15 minutes into the flight, Raffaele hijacked the plane, demanding they head towards New York. He easily gained access to the cockpit. All on board soon heard Captain Donald Cook announce, "We have a nervous young man up here and we are going to take him wherever he wants to go." Most on board thought they'd be heading to Cuba, which had long been a hijacker destination of choice. In fact, most US airlines provided their captains Caribbean maps in case they unexpectedly had to fly to Havana. Still, others on board heard rumors of a destination in faraway places such as Egypt and Italy. Eventually Raffaele allowed the pilot to speak with the passengers again: "If you've made plans in San Francisco, don't plan on keeping them. Because we're going to New York." Captain Cook knew the problem, the plane had only enough fuel for its shorter planned trip. Two hours and thirty-three minutes into the hijacking, Minichiello finally allowed the plane to land in Denver to refuel. He then surprised everyone by allowing all 39 other passengers and three flight attendants off the plane during refueling. Now refueled, and with only five people on board including Raffaele, the plane continued to New York, arriving six hours and 51 minutes into the hijacking.

At JFK International Airport, the FBI had almost one hundred agents ready, some disguised as mechanics. Though Raffaele had warned that no one should approach the plane as it parked far away from the terminal, he was nervously pacing the plane fearing someone would shoot him if he approached a window. The pilot, seeing the agents approaching, warned them to stay back. Suddenly, a shot rang out. Minichiello hadn't intended to shoot but, just outside the cockpit door, he accidentally fired his weapon. The bullet pierced the ceiling and

glanced off an oxygen tank, neither piercing it nor the plane's fuselage. Had the shot damaged the latter, the plane couldn't have continued to fly. If the bullet had ruptured the oxygen tank the explosion likely would've destroyed the plane and everyone aboard. The captain, sure that Minichiello purposely fired the rifle behind him, yelled for agents to withdraw, adding the plane would be taking off again without refueling. Two waiting TWA captains who were cleared to fly internationally (as Captain Cook was not) pushed their way through the FBI agents and boarded the plane. The plane now left with nowhere near enough fuel to reach its international destination of Rome.

Seven hours and 25 minutes into the hijacking, the plane turned towards the small airport of Bangor Maine to try another refueling before crossing the Atlantic Ocean. Captain Cook, who remained on board, convinced Raffaele the crew hadn't been party to the chaos and problems at JFK. The media frenzy continued with reporters and photographers flocking to Bangor's airport. About 75 police officers were necessary to keep the press as far away as possible. Captain Cook radioed the control tower to have a couple of people removed from a nearby building after Minichiello spotted them from the plane: "You had better hurry. He says he is going to start shooting at that building unless they get a move on."

Now fueled for the trans-Atlantic crossing, the plane left Bangor for international airspace at nine hours and seven minutes into the hijacking. Though trying to keep Raffaele happy, the crew continuously feared for their lives. Cook even lied to him, saying that he was married with a child, in hopes that he'd be less likely to shoot him. Six hours later, the plane landed in Shannon, Ireland, again to refuel. On approach to Ireland, TWA85 crossed time zones and it became November 1 – Raffaele's birthday. The hijacker had turned twenty years old. Uneventfully, the plane left Ireland for its planned end-stop in Rome.

As the plane neared Rome's Fiumicino airport in the early morning, Minichiello demanded an unarmed police official meet the plane far from the terminal when they landed. Pietro Guli, a deputy customs official volunteered to be that man. Eighteen and half hours after it began, and 6,900 miles (11,000 kilometers) later, Raffaele walked off the plane, casually apologizing to Captain Cook for all the trouble he gave them. He now had a new hostage, Pietro Guli. Raffaele ordered his hostage to take him south to Naples – he was heading home. Four police cars trailed them on the way. Minichiello's captive carefully followed the directions he gave until they had somehow evaded the accompanying vehicles. Yet, after making a mistake with his directions Raffaele unintentionally reached a dead end. Realizing his limited choices, he now ran on foot. Over five hours of a manhunt in the hills, with hundreds of officers, a few helicopters and some dogs, they didn't find him. It was a priest who discovered him at All Saint's Day morning service, recognizing him as he tried to blend in. This priest called the police and Raffaele's journey came to end 23 hours after leaving Los Angeles.

Minichiello would have faced the death penalty if returned to the US, which American authorities now sought. Unbelievably, Italians rallied around him. They portrayed him as a fresh-faced uncultured peasant Italian boy who was a victim of a horrible foreign war, a good boy who would do anything to return to the motherland. He became a folk hero in Italy, not the potentially murderous gun waving hijacker who threatened a planeload of passengers. Arresting authorities quickly said he would face trial only in Italy.

In the end, Italy only prosecuted him for crimes committed in the country and in their airspace and sentenced him to a seven-and-a-half-year prison term. Lawyers quickly and successfully appealed that sentence. They released Raffaele on May 1, 1971. The 21-year-old was again a free man, one without regret for his earlier actions.

Minichiello tried to use his fame and notoriety, yet his nude modeling career and promised film career in Westerns each failed. He started working as a bartender in Rome, later marrying the bar owner's daughter, Cinzia, with whom he had a son. They later started a pizza restaurant called Hijacking.

Cinzia became pregnant with their second child. In February 1985, she was admitted to a hospital while in labor. Cinzia and her newborn son both died because of medical malpractice. Raffaele, once again, was angry with authorities. This time he plotted revenge by planning to attack a prominent medical conference near Rome. In his mind, this would draw attention to the official negligence that lost him his wife and son. He bought the guns he needed for his attack. During this dark rage, Tony, a colleague, started a friendship with Raffaele. Tony recognized the distress Raffaele was in and introduced him to the Bible. As a Christian, Tony would select and read him passages. And Raffaele listened. Over time, God softened Raffaele's heart and he too became a believer. It was then that he called off his planned attack.

In 1999, Raffaele decided to return to the United States for the first time since his hijacking. He learned that all outstanding criminal charges no longer existed but that he had received an "other than honorable discharge" by the Marines due to his fleeing his court martial. One thing he wanted to do in returning to the US was apologize to those he had held captive years earlier, if they would meet with him. It took him until August of 2009 to accomplish this. One flight attendant and the first officer, Wenzel Williams, were the only ones who agreed. It especially hurt Raffaele that Captain Cook refused. Williams found Raffaele a different person, one weighed by his guilt and someone with sincere remorse. This former thief, deserter, and perpetrator of what the New York Times called "the world's longest and most spectacular hijacking," was now a changed believer in Jesus Christ. Minichiello handed both his former captives a gift as they left. They were New Testaments. Inside he wrote: "Thank you for your time, so much. I appreciate your forgiveness for my actions that put you in harm's way. Please accept this book, that has changed my life. God bless you so much, Raffaele Minichiello." Underneath he added "Luke 23:34."

Would you welcome this man in your church? Unlike every other person studied in this book, this contact is a real possibility. Though elderly, at the time of writing, this brother in Christ is still alive and living outside Naples.

# Chapter Eleven

## What Will You Do?

In these brief stories you've met some of the worst of humanity. These were murderers, human traffickers, terrorists, hijackers, perverts, state oppressors, liars and thieves. Overall, most never faced human justice for their crimes, never spending a day in jail for their offenses. If their names and actions made today's news, the cry would be unending. It doesn't matter what they later became, believe, or did. It doesn't matter how much contrition they've shown. They still deserve to face justice and banishment from society. Social justice demands that all aware of their earlier deeds must forever shun them. If *you* refuse to denounce them or choose to work or socialize with them, you *must* agree with all they've done. Any church welcoming them for fellowship and worship faces the same accusation. Their mere presence in your gathering means you excuse all that they once stood for. In the face of this public scorn, what would you do today when such a man or woman comes into your life or congregation?

If you believe that God sent Jesus to save the worst of sinners, you must believe that God can and does change hearts and minds. He's in the business of transformed lives. It's easy to pay lip service to this idea, but you'll prove your true understanding by your actions.

You'll verify your love for Him by your love and

acceptance of your brothers and sisters in the faith.[175] This especially includes the ones that are nothing like you and specifically the ones who once disgusted you. Could you rejoice if a sinner as vile as Adolph Hitler or Joseph Stalin repented and believed? Do you want to see the worst person you know of come to faith in Jesus Christ *and* join you in friendship and worship?

**John 15:12** "This is my commandment, that you love one another as I have loved you.

I praise God for his saints, men and women, throughout history who were willing to identify with these vile people who repented of their former sinfulness and odious actions. I thank God they didn't wait until those people were perfect. Rather they came alongside them even as they were learning what it meant to be a follower of Jesus Christ and not all their beliefs yet conformed to God's word. I thank God that some of these same Godly people came alongside me. For I too was a sinner justifying my evil thoughts and deeds before Jesus saved  me.[176] As a newly committed Christ follower, I didn't change overnight; I still had much to learn. I proved this by my wrong actions and years of often ill-informed beliefs. In this weakness, God had His people who were willing to identify with me, a former sinner now a saint struggling to no longer sin.

**1 Timothy 1:15** This *is* a faithful saying, and worthy of all acceptation, that Christ Jesus came into the world to save

---

[175] See John 14:15, 24.

[176] And, yes, you can grow up attending a Bible-believing church without being a believer.

sinners; of whom I am chief.

On that day you meet your Savior, do you hope Jesus will introduce you to the people you've met in the pages of this book? Do you hope He'll say, "come and meet these brothers and sister of yours?" I look forward to meeting each and all these vile sinners now radically saved and transformed by God's amazing grace. I long to hear their stories of God's forgiveness and boundless grace. Multitudes of these of these "forever unforgiveable" but now transformed people will fill heaven and rejoice around God's throne. Redeemed and Forgiven![177]

---

[177] Colossians 1:13 He has delivered us from the domain of darkness and transferred us to the kingdom of his beloved Son, 14 in whom we have redemption, the forgiveness of sins.

Photographs and Illustrations

Cover design by: Emma Elzinga

P. 14 – Statue with Roman armor, Bergama Museum, Turkey. Photo by author, 2011.

P. 18 – Statue Roman Emperor Hadrian, Antalya Museum, Antalya, Turkey. Photo by author, 2011.

P. 22 – Ship Diagram, Ephraim Chambers Cyclopedia, 1728. Public Domain.

P. 23 – 19th century drawing of John Newton. Public Domain.

P. 25 – St. Anne's Church, St. Kitts. Photo by author, 2017.

P. 25 – Letter excerpt, Amazing Grace Experience, St. Kitts. Photo by author, 2017.

P. 27 – Epitaph, Amazing Grace Experience, St. Kitts. Photo by author, 2017.

P. 30 – Lt. Gen. Nathan Bedford Forrest, Confederate States Army. Library of Congress. Public Domain.

P. 31 – 1901 Nathan Bedford Forrest statue in Forrest Park, later renamed Health Sciences Park in 2013, Memphis, TN. Forrest and his wife were reburied in front of this monument in 1904. The city sold the park for a nominal sum enabling removal of the statue in December of 2017. Public Domain.

P. 32 – Nathan Bedford Forrest Bust at State Capitol, Nashville, TN. 2019. Public Domain.

P. 33 – Illustration, Klansmen trying to lynch a carpetbagger in 1871. Public Domain.

P. 34 – Reverend G. T. Stainback, D.D., 1905, Public Domain per Wikipedia

P. 38 – The Samaritan Scrolls (cropped), 1905, Public Domain per Wikipedia.

P. 40 – Statue of Nemesis, Antalya Museum, Antalya, Turkey. Photo by author, 2011.

P. 42 – Roman floor mosaic with chi-rho and alpha & omega, Sousse Archaeological Museum, Sousse, Tunisia. Photo by author, 2017.

P. 43 – Byzantine baptismal font at Bardo Museum, Tunis, Tunisia. Photo by author, 2017.

P. 44 – Roman bust from ancient Smyrna, Izmir, Turkey. Photo by author, 2015.

P. 45 – Relief on Arch of Constantine, Rome, Italy. Photo by author, 2010.

P. 46 – Gold solidus coin featuring Julian The Apostate. Public Domain.

P. 46 – Olympian gods of the Parthenon frieze at British Museum, London, England. Photo by author, 2012.

P. 47 – Roman period jewelry at Bergama Museum, Pergamum, Turkey. Photo by author, 2011.

P. 48 – Floor mosaic, "Ceremonial dressing of a lady," at Bardo Museum, Tunis, Tunisia. Photo by author, 2017.

P. 48 – Bronze head of woman with eyes having silver inlay, at British Museum, London, England. Photo by author, 2012.

P. 49 – Early Roman period "Head of a woman," from Pergamon, at Izmir Museum, Izmir, Turkey. Photo by author, 2011.

P. 51 – Giza Pyramids. Photo by author, 2018.

P. 52 – Statue of Jerome at the Church of Saint Catherine of Alexandria, connected to the Church of the Nativity, Bethlehem, Israel. Photo by author, 2011.

P. 53 – Codex Amiatinus, Genesis (first page), Carta ii r from Biblioteca Medicea Laurenziana (the Laurentian Library, http://mss.bmlonline.it/) in Florence, Italy. Retrieved 2019.

P. 55 – Trove of silver coins, "The Treasure of Side," at the Antalya Museum, Antalya, Turkey. Photo by author, 2011.

P. 60 – Model of Jerusalem temple at the Israel Museum, Jerusalem, Israel. Photo by author, 2013.

P. 61 – Photo of Arbel cliffs, Israel. Photo by author, 2015.

P. 63 – Statues of Roman period woman, Beirut, Lebanon. Photo by author, 2013.

P. 64 – Rolling stone tomb at the Sisters of Zion Convent, Nazareth, Israel. Photo by author, 2015.

P. 66 – Ka'ahumanu, "Reine Cahoumanou," Plate III in Louis Choris' Voyage Pittoresque Autour du Monde, Paris, 1822, Hawaii State Archives. Public Domain.

P. 67 – View of Ka'awaloa, Kealakekua Bay, drawn by Persis, daughter of Lucy and Asa Thurston, 1835. Public Domain.

P. 68 – Reverend Hiram Bingham, from his book, A Residence of Twenty-One Years in the Sandwich Islands, published in 1848. Public Domain.

P. 69 – Kawaiahao Church illustration, c. 1870s. Public Domain.

P. 70 – Cover page of Hawaiian Bible Palapala Hemolele, 1838 edition. Public Domain.

P. 72 – Jeffrey Dahmer yearbook photo. Publicly circulated. Fair Use.

P. 73 – Jeffrey Dahmer Milwaukee County mug shot. Publicly circulated. Fair Use.

P. 76 – Jeffrey Dahmer Milwaukee mug shot with glasses. Publicly circulated. Fair Use.

P. 82 – Roman period bust of a man at Bergama Museum, Pergamum, Turkey. Photo by author, 2011.

P. 86 – Black goat at Petra, Jordan. Photo by author, 2018.

P. 93 – Roman floor mosaic of a ship, Sousse Archaeological Museum, Sousse, Tunisia. Photo by author, 2017.

P. 94 – Painting "Saint Paul Writing His Epistles," attributed to Valentin de Boulogne (1591-1632). Public Domain.

P. 98 – Byang Kato at SIM Senior Primary School, 1954, as published in *Byang Kato: Ambassador for Christ* by Sophie de la Haye, African Christian Press, 1986. Fair Use.

P. 100 – Portrait of Byang Kato, date unknown, as published in *Byang Kato: Ambassador for Christ* by Sophie de la Haye, African Christian Press, 1986. Fair Use.

P. 102 – Raffaele Minichiello Vietnam war photos, unknown date. Publicly circulated. Fair Use.

P. 104 – TWA highjack plane, OCT.-31-1969-BANGOR-INTERNATIONAL-AIRPORT-HIJACKED-BOEING - Jack Loftus Bangor Daily News. Fair Use.

P. 106 – Raffaele Minichiello enters Rome police headquarters after he was arrested Nov. 1, 1969, Associated Press News. Fair Use.

P. 107 – Raffaele Minichiello in Rome, unknown date (used on https://skyjackeroftheday.tumblr.com/). Retrieved 2019. Fair Use.

P. 110 – Forgiveness graphic. By author, 2020.

# ABOUT THE AUTHOR

Brent J. MacDonald is a pastor, teacher, and bible researcher with a focus on biblical archaeology and the historicity of bible events. As executive director of Cottage Cove Urban Ministries in Nashville, Tennessee – a ministry for at-risk children and youth – he enables and encourages people to live out lives of love for "the least of these." Brent frequently travels with his wife Angie for on-site research in the Bible lands.

# ABOUT KHARIS PUBLISHING

Kharis Publishing, an imprint of Kharis Media LLC, is a leading inspirational and faith publisher with a core mission to publish impactful books, and support at-risk children with literacy tools. Kharis Publishing is committed to giving voice to under-represented writers, including women and first-time authors. Learn more at www.kharispublishing.com.

CPSIA information can be obtained
at www.ICGtesting.com
Printed in the USA
FSHW020305060920
73592FS